THE CAMBRIDGE MISCELLANY

IV

TWO SAINTS

TWO SAINTS:
ST BERNARD & ST FRANCIS

G. G. COULTON

AT THE UNIVERSITY PRESS

1932

To

PROFESSOR J. P. WHITNEY
In friendship and respect

CAMBRIDGE UNIVERSITY PRESS
Cambridge, New York, Melbourne, Madrid, Cape Town,
Singapore, São Paulo, Delhi, Tokyo, Mexico City

Cambridge University Press
The Edinburgh Building, Cambridge CB2 8RU, UK

Published in the United States of America by Cambridge University Press, New York

www.cambridge.org
Information on this title: www.cambridge.org/9781107633230

First published 1932
First paperback edition 2011

A catalogue record for this publication is available from the British Library

ISBN 978-1-107-63323-0 Paperback

CONTENTS

ILLUSTRATIONS

PREFACE

I HAVE more than once been asked to reprint separately the Bernardine chapters from the first volume of *Five Centuries of Religion*; and to these I now add the corresponding Franciscan chapters from the second volume. A few words have been added, and nearly all the footnotes and references have been cut out from these reprints, since they are available in the complete volumes, and even those critics who have most strongly dissented from some of my conclusions have admitted the general accuracy of my references. For the index to this, as to other volumes, I am indebted to my wife.

G. G. C.

ST JOHN'S COLLEGE
CAMBRIDGE
May 1932

CHAPTER I

ST BERNARD

S T BERNARD'S fame has perhaps been too much overshadowed in recent years by that of St Francis of Assisi. He has also suffered through his quarrel with Abailard, though here he only kept up the traditions of his Order,[1] and defended a conservative position in theology which was destined soon to be swept away by the rise of the universities. It is true that, on all the main points at issue between the two men, the ablest and most orthodox churchmen of the next century tacitly decided against St Bernard. Not only were Abailard's main philosophical positions triumphant, but his root-principle triumphed, that revealed religion must be busily and constantly supported by reason. The great scholastic philosophers derive not from Bernard but from Abailard. As Rashdall has said:

To men like St Bernard the *Summa Theologiae* of St Thomas, with its full statement of objections and free discussion of difficulties, would have

[1] *I.e.* of the Benedictines. It must be remembered that neither Cluniac nor Cistercian had any other Rule than Benedict's though each had his distinctive *consuetudines*— by-laws or customs.

seemed as shocking an exhibition of human pride and intellectual self-sufficiency as the *Theologia* of Abelard.

It may be said, in fact, that what most offended the saint was the idea that there should be a philosophy of religion at all; he fought against the application of strict logical methods to revealed religion, even in its support. Here he followed what was tacitly, if not expressly, the general Benedictine tradition; and his position helps us to understand why the Benedictines had practically nothing to do with the founding of universities; why they scarcely ever supplied teachers to those universities, once founded; and why they appeared there, even as scholars, so tardily, so seldom and so reluctantly. In 1244, when another English Stephen, abbot of Clairvaux, founded a Cistercian college at Paris which was called after St Bernard, this was certainly an unconstitutional act; even the pope's support did not save the new movement from much criticism; and Stephen's deposition in 1255 is ascribed by Matthew Paris to the unpopularity which he thus incurred.

Disastrous, again, was that Second Crusade in which St Bernard interested himself so directly; and there were other failures mingled with his great political successes outside the cloister. But here it would be most unjust to lay anything whatever to the charge of the man who asked for nothing more than to be left undisturbed in his beloved Clairvaux. No man ever strove harder for worldly success than Bernard strove for retirement; and, of all his heavy sacrifices, assuredly the greatest was his frequent obedience to the call of popes or prelates who needed his help, and who thus drew him away from mortification, silence and prayer. It is as a monk that Bernard should be judged; for he would never willingly have said or done anything outside his narrowest monastic duties; his whole extra-claustral work was a charitable concession to the necessities of other men, or of the Church which he loved even more than his own community. In spirit, he was nothing but a monk, and in that spirit alone are we here concerned with him. We may thus be better able to realize why later writers looked up to him as the Fifth Doctor of the Church; why (as Vacandard points out) much of the *Imitatio* is borrowed from his writings; and why even Luther paid him a tribute which he vouchsafed to very few medieval writers. A generation which knows Bernard mainly through his extra-claustral activities, and therefore sees in him the maker and unmaker of popes, the organizer of a crusade, and the enemy of Abailard and Arnold of Brescia, is a generation which does him great injustice.

Few men ever brought to the service of an ideal, chosen so early and unflinchingly, a nobler combination of qualities. Francis was born of the merchant nobility, Bernard sprang from the fighting caste. He was born at the castle of Fontaine near Dijon, on that hill where the orphanage

Fig. 1. Fontaine-les-Dijon from the Vineyards.

stands now. The castle is gone, though its inner and outer bailey may still be traced; even the little chapel has been replaced by a later medieval church; but the eternal hills stand as they stood in Bernard's time. The village street still winds steeply upward; and the pilgrim who has walked the short three miles from Dijon finds his labour

4

well rewarded. From the castle knoll we look straight across to the rival hill-village of Talant with its wonderful church, and sideways down upon the great city; and thence again, over the plain of Burgundy, to the blue line of Jura and those magical subalpine marches which Ruskin has immortalized. At our feet are the vineyards, rooted in a rich soil which turns orange-brown to the sun, and alternating with even richer orchards; here we have "la vraie Bourgogne, l'aimable et vineuse Bourgogne, où tout le monde s'appelle frère ou cousin; pays de bons vivants et des joyeux noël". Bernard's mother, descended from the ancient dukes of Burgundy, came from that castle of Montbard which is now famous as Buffon's home. His father was one of the most trusted vassals of the count of Burgundy; it was noted that this prince had never lost a battle in which Tescelin *li Sors* had fought by his side. The very surname is significant; Tescelin the Tawny-haired was a descendant of the conquering race; yellow-brown or yellow are very rare shades in modern Dijon, as the traveller may easily see for himself in street or theatre or church. Bernard, then, though French in culture, was Burgundian by race; less truly a child of the southern sun than of the great northern forests; his fair hair and transparent skin and slender figure speak for that. No peoples were so suddenly or so thoroughly Christianized as these northern invaders. The refinements of thought which had troubled Origen and Augustine, or those which were destined to trouble Pascal and Newman in later days, slept among the vast multitude in the twelfth century. There was an all-embracing Church, ubiquitous, most visible and sensible and audible; unrivalled, if only because it suffered no rival; the natural refuge, with almost negligible exceptions, for all men who were attracted by learning or faith or discipline. To the simple mind, it held out attractions almost as tangible as the rudimentary rites of paganism; to the enquirer, it offered ineffable mysteries. Thus equipped, it conquered all the conquerors in turn: Goth, Vandal, Burgundian, Frank, Lombard and Norman. But the latest arrivals came most suddenly and completely to the Church; whether because these maturer minds were ripe for a complete conversion, or because the more feudalized pagans found a semi-feudal, semi-pagan Church to welcome them, to teach them, and at the same time to grow up with them, like an early-married mother with her child.

This Fontaine family had high traditions of uprightness and piety. Bernard's own personal beauty was remarkable from childhood; and of his appearance in later life we have one precious description which brings him nearer to us, perhaps, than any other man of his century.

His body (writes one who knew him well) was marked by a certain grace rather spiritual than corporeal; his face was radiant with a light not of earth but of heaven; his eyes shone with angelic purity and dovelike simplicity. Such was the beauty of the inner man, that it brake forth by manifest tokens to the sight, and even the outer man seemed bedewed with the abundance of his inward purity and grace. His whole body was meagre and emaciated. His skin itself was of the finest texture, with a slight flush of red on the cheeks, seeing that all the natural heat of his frame had been drawn thither by constant meditation and the zeal of his holy compunction. His hair was of a yellow inclining to white; his beard was auburn, sprinkled towards the end of his life with grey. His stature was of an honourable middle size, yet inclining to tallness.

This set description is borne out by other uncalculated touches which come out in the biographies. For, here again, Bernard was fortunate in the number and fulness of his contemporary or sub-contemporary biographers; or (shall we say) his greatness created a whole biographical cycle. One, recording the saint's answer to one of his own questions, notes the habitual charm of his smile; another tells how the saint met a heretic of Languedoc, who, anxious to discount the effect of

St Bernard's discourses, came up to him as he mounted his horse to depart,

and, raising his head, cried aloud in the hearing of all men: "My lord abbot, know that the horse of our master, whom ye paint in such evil colours, is not so fat and well-liking as this good steed of yours". The saint answered mildly and patiently, without change of face or mind: "I confess, friend, that thou sayest truth. Yet thou must know that this beast which thou castest in my teeth is a senseless animal, of those which nature hath formed to bow his head and to obey his belly; wherefore, if he eateth his fill and waxeth fat, therein is no injustice nor offence to God, for the horse liveth after his own fashion. But I and thy master, before God's judgement-seat, shall not be arraigned according to our horses' necks; nay, each shall be judged for his own. Now, therefore, may it please you to consider my neck and to see whether it be grosser than that of thy master, so as to lend justice, perchance, to thy rebuke?" Thus saying, he cast back his cowl and bared his head to the shoulders, displaying his long and slender neck; which, thin and emaciated as it was, yet by heaven's grace it was as white and comely as that of a swan; so that all who stood by rejoiced with great joy at this sight, and blessed the Lord God who had put into His servant's mouth so ready and just an answer, to the confusion and stopping of the mouth that spake wicked things.

And let us not forget that in one most important respect he rose definitely above his age and his environment; amid all his mortifications he repudiated the idea of exalting personal neglect or uncleanliness into a monastic virtue.

His mother suckled all her seven children herself: "the noble lady disdained to commit them

Fig. 2. A Medieval Nurse (*c.* 1300).

to another's breasts, but infused into them something of her own goodness with this mother's milk". She brought her sons up to plain living even in a noble household; Bernard was the third in age. Of his boyhood little is recorded but his purity, his love of meditation, and his violent headaches. He gained rapid proficiency in Latin letters; and Abailard's friend Bérenger of Poitiers cast it in his teeth that he had been a precocious poet. Literary ambitions naturally attracted him; but in his home he had already taken too strong a tinge of that faith which compels a man to choose between time and eternity. One day in the autumn of 1111, at the age of 21, he turned aside as usual to pray by himself in a little wayside church. In that hour the agony of conversion came upon him; *haec est mutatio dexterae Excelsi*; there, before the altar, he "poured forth his soul like water", and thenceforth his vocation was irrevocably fixed. After an apprenticeship of six months at the priory of Châtillon-sur-Seine, he came to Cîteaux in the spring of 1112, bringing with him twenty-nine other *nobiles aut litterati*. Thenceforward he would constantly remind himself that "the road winds uphill all the way—yea, to the very end". *Bernarde, ad quid venisti?*—"What are you here for?" "To be crucified with Christ." He lived to see father, mother, sister and all five brothers in the cloister, mainly through his own example. One brother left his knighthood in the world; another persuaded his wife to share his sacrifice and to take the veil when he took the frock. Nivard, the youngest, was still "a boy playing with his fellows in the village street", when he was fired by

Bernard's example. For once, the saint faltered, and counselled the child rather to take up his father's office and inheritance. "It is not just", replied Nivard, "that ye all should take heaven to yourselves and leave the world to me"; and, as soon as his age permitted, he took the vows. By this time Bernard was already abbot; for Cîteaux, which at his accession had been so near to despair, grew so rapidly from that time forward that it threw out three new colonies in two years; and with the third of these, Clairvaux, Bernard himself was sent in command. He lived to see 350 abbeys, with 150 dependent cells, in the Order; within 50 years of his death it was one of the greatest of European institutions, with 530 abbeys and more than 650 dependencies. For here was a man as business-like as Stephen Harding, that Sherborne man who did so much for the foundation of the Cistercian Order, but with the soul of a knight and poet to boot; fitted to be an intellectual leader in his age, but far more exceptional in character than in intellect. He had the fearless resolution of his race; the physical fearlessness of a Nelson, never counting the odds, but seeing at a glance where the chances of victory lay, and attacking with that swift and instinctive directness which itself is half success. St Catharine of Siena spoke plainly enough to the popes and great men of her time, if only she could have left it there; but, at the end of her bitterest and most merited rebukes, she too often threw herself almost grovelling at the pontiff's feet—"pardon my presumption, that I presume to write to you"—"pardon, Father, my ignorance"—"pardon me, pardon me!" St Bernard laid the stripes on with equal directness, and left them to smart. "This servant of God (says one biographer) was eminent above all men in liberty of spirit, yet with humility and mildness, so that he seemed as it were to fear no man and to reverence all men." To the pope he writes:

I speak with confidence because I love with fidelity.... There is one voice among all who rule their flocks here with faithful care—that justice is perishing in the Church, the keys of the Church are being set at nought.... They impute the cause of this to you and the Roman Court.... In writing this, I should fear to be branded for presumption, if I knew not who you are to whom I write, and who am I that write. But I know your natural mildness, and I know that you know me, and the affection with which I dare to write you these words, sweetest and most loving Father.

And again, to Eugenius III, after painting the court of Rome as a sink of litigation and unjust appeals, he says plainly: "If thou art Christ's disciple, let thy zeal be kindled and let thine

authority rise up against this shamelessness". Nor
was he less plain spoken to the great men of the
world. To Louis VII he wrote:

From whom, but from the devil, can I say that
this policy of yours proceeds?...your advisers in
this matter seek not your honour but their own
profit—nay, the devil's will....Whatsoever it may
please you to do with your own realm and crown
and soul, we, as sons of the Church, cannot hold
our peace in face of the insults and contempt with
which our Mother is trodden underfoot.

To this he added moral courage; few men have
been strong enough to stand so stiffly upon the
ground they had once chosen, yet so constantly
mindful of that Pauline warning: "let him that
thinketh he standeth take heed lest he fall".
Courage, again, was required beyond ordinary
measure for the mortifications which Bernard accepted as the duty of his profession. The fasts,
severe in any case and cruelly exaggerated by this
man who had come "to be crucified with Christ";
the coarse food, fit enough for a peasant but un-
suited to a frame which had become too emaciated
for severe manual work, and was wasted still
thinner by constant wear of mind and spirit; the
nightly vigils; all combined to ruin his digestion.
He lost all taste for food; once he drank oil by
mistake for wine; water was the only thing for
which he had a real appetite, since it cooled his

inflamed throat. His stomach often rejected all nourishment; at those times he was unable to go into choir with the brethren, but waited at the door and followed their service at a distance. By a pathetic revenge of nature, he was at last compelled unwillingly to accept valetudinarian indulgences; and Étienne de Bourbon tells us how Louis VII's messengers, bringing a present of fish to St Bernard in his later days, found him in the infirmary before a roast capon.

The King, unable to believe this of so great a saint, told him in familiar speech of his messengers' report. St Bernard confessed that this was true; since, so long as he was in health and had felt his bodily force sufficient to endure, he had worn it down with abstinences; so that this body, unable to bear any longer those burdens, must now be borne and sustained itself; unto which his superior constrained him. The King, hearing this, was edified.

Bernard's writings testify, almost involuntarily, to his naturally keen observation and sense of beauty; yet these he resolutely repressed as hindrances to his vocation. In the novice-room at Cîteaux, in which his whole first year was spent, he never noticed the vault; nor did he know whether the eastern wall of the church had a single or a triple window. After a day's ride along the Lake of Geneva, he astounded his companions by betraying complete ignorance that any such water had been within their sight. Therefore it is natural that, with all his literary capacities and his earlier literary attainments, he should show himself rather, in after life, as a man of one book. He quotes Virgil and Ovid, Ambrose, Augustine and Gregory; Jerome less frequently; Origen's commentaries he knew; but his real literary force is in his knowledge of the Bible text. It was once a Protestant superstition that no Catholic ever knew his Bible well. For all English-speaking people who take the trouble to get at the facts, that legend was finally destroyed in S. R. Maitland's *Dark Ages*; but Maitland leaves room for, without himself propagating, an equally false legend on the other side. The rough truth may be put very simply; the best medieval writers knew their Vulgate very well; a great many more knew parts of it well enough, especially those portions which happened to come in their service-books. The average priest knew nothing outside those service-books, and not even all that was inside; the lower priesthood, as Roger Bacon and other equally credible witnesses testify, understood little or nothing even of their church offices. The laity could seldom read Latin with any ease, beyond the sort of hotel-waiter's vocabulary with which a few men wrote their accounts or a scrivener his legal formulae; therefore the most educated and ambitious seldom got far beyond the Psalms and the Sunday Gospels and Epistles. A few of the richest possessed Bibles in French or Psalters in French or English; but, as soon as a general desire for vernacular translation arose, this was opposed by the ecclesiastical authorities, and for the rest of the Middle Ages vernacular Bibles were either explicitly condemned, or lay under a strong suspicion of heresy. So strongly did the Church in general disapprove of vernacular religious books on the whole, that this reason has been plausibly urged to account for the extraordinarily small circulation of the French translation which was made, at a very early date, from some of St Bernard's sermons. But Bernard himself, as we have said, knew his Bible inside and out; Luther and Bunyan knew it no better. He had conned it a thousand times over in lonely meditation and made the whole book his own; and this is how we must explain that saying of his, that his best teachers had been the oaks and the beeches; reading and meditation in the forest round Clairvaux. The Bible became bone of his bone and flesh of his flesh. Thus men noted that, when he spoke from the Bible, it was as if he were composing, and not repeating; as if the Holy Ghost were speaking directly from his mouth. Some men will still remember how the late Dean Vaughan was accustomed to read the Pauline epistles with a quiet depth of conviction, and an exact justice of emphasis born of lifelong study, which gave the impression that he himself was reasoning with the congregation in his own words, rather than rehearsing those of another. The legend of Bernard's Bible-knowledge was living down to the end of the Middle Ages, as we may see in the 4th chapter of the *Praise of Folly*. Erasmus there alludes to the story that Satan tempted the saint, boasting how he could tell him seven verses of the Psalms which, recited daily, would lead the soul infallibly to heaven. To this St Bernard answered that he would recite the whole Psalter daily, and therefore needed no supernatural help in selection.

Vaughan, with his other qualities, had the keenest eye for human foibles; and so had Bernard. It would be difficult to find any more effective satire in medieval literature than we can find occasionally in his letters, and even in his sermons. To those who pleaded Paul's advice to Timothy that he should not stint himself with wine, Bernard replied: "Show me a Timothy, and I will feed him on gold if you will, and give him balsam to drink!" He was pitiless in scorn of those monks who were solicitous about the dignity of their dress, or who needed beautiful churches to stimulate their devotion. From Bernard's letters to the abbey of

St-Germer de Fly, the abbey where Guibert of Nogent had passed his earlier monastic years, Gibbon might have learned, as he learned from Pascal, "to wield the weapon of grave and temperate irony" (Epp. 67, 68). And Bernard strove to keep his inner eye as clear as the outer. "He was wont, from his own experience, to define a wise man as one to whom all things taste even as they really are—*sapiens, cui omnia sapiunt sicut sunt*." He loved that text from 1 Cor. xiv, 38, Vulg.: *si quis ignorat, ignorabitur*—he who ignores, shall be ignored by God. The one occasion on which he fell very definitely short of this ideal has been recounted with perhaps a little exaggeration of emphasis by J. C. Morison in his *Life of St Bernard*; but the lapse itself is frankly admitted by Abbé Vacandard. St Bernard there adopted a crooked policy; he recommended the pope to let their enemy perish in his own inventions; and the result brought merited difficulties upon pope, saint and Church.

With his usually direct outward and inward vision accords his ruling common-sense. When the canons of the great cathedral of Lyons attempted to popularize the idea of the Immaculate Conception of the Virgin Mary, it was Bernard who most definitely withstood them, though his personal devotion to her was extreme, and the

Cistercians claimed in a special sense to be Children of Mary. It was that letter of his which did more than any other single thing to postpone the final proclamation of the dogma until 1854; so that some fervent Mariolaters of the later Middle Ages did not hesitate to preach that the saint bore an eternal spot on his breast in heaven, to atone for his share in this dispute. His treatise *De Praecepto et Dispensatione* is a model of judicial discussion on thorny points of claustral casuistry. Very significant, again, is his love of the word *ordo*, his overwhelming sense of the social side of religion, and the eagerness with which he catches at this word, in the Bible, to emphasize the necessity of co-operation and discipline and subordination even in the struggle for personal salvation—the value, not only of the individual effort, but also of all that made him ready to sacrifice himself for his own Cistercian Order. In Book v of his *De Consideratione*, § 20, he comes to speak to the pope of those unclerical clerics who swarmed even in the twelfth century, and who too often took the best places.

These men neither fight as knights, nor preach the gospel as clerics. Of what order, then, are they?...It is written concerning the resurrection from the dead, "Every man in his own order"; in what order, then, shall these men rise?...I fear lest they find themselves, on that day, in that place whereof Job speaketh: "A land of darkness, as darkness itself, and of the shadows of death, without any order, and where the light is darkness".

The world, the natural world, is disorder; the soul that is to be saved must order itself by stern renunciation and self-control. Where, in Isaiah xxx, 15, the Authorized Version has "in quietness and in confidence shall be your strength", the Vulgate reads "in silentio et in spe erit fortitudo vestra"—in silence and in hope. That text was always in Bernard's mind; and by that he ordered his life; the silence was the silence of the monastery, the "taciturnitas" of the Order, prescribed 600 years earlier by St Benedict; and hope was the lawful portion of every true Benedictine; a hope that maketh not ashamed.

Bernard's character comes out most clearly in his letters, which are certainly among the most intimate documents of the Middle Ages. In them, the art of a writer who had profited by his classical training never obscures his deep and intense feeling; he writes far more directly than the average of his contemporaries; and this correspondence, by itself, would suffice to show us why Dante's infallible eye pitched upon charity as the saint's distinguishing characteristic: *la vivace carità di colui*. He was among the few who protested most publicly against the massacres of Jews which accompanied the enthusiasm of the Second Crusade; he made no attempt to excite the populace to the burning of heretics; for, in those days, such *autos-da-fé* were rather popular than official, and the mob was only too ready to persecute whenever any influential churchman gave the word. As abbot of Clairvaux for nearly forty years, at a time when that monastery was not only living its own life, but serving as a huge seminary for the whole Order, he must have had literally thousands of converts through his hands; and, while making all allowance for the biographers' temptations to exaggerate, we wonder far more at the permanence of Bernard's influence than at its immediate effect. Dr Arnold (Dean Stanley tells us) would say that "it was the first, second, and third duty of a schoolmaster to get rid of unpromising subjects". St Bernard rose above this stern principle; the Lake of Geneva he could ignore, but never the least need of his spiritual children, "the babes whom I have brought forth in the Gospel". In the preface to his *De Consideratione*, he addresses his former pupil, Eugenius III, now raised to the papacy, and insists upon this unbroken bond.

Hast thou mounted upon Peter's throne? Though thou shouldest walk on the wings of the wind, yet shalt thou not escape from my affection. I have lost the duty of a mother towards thee; but no man shall deprive me of the mother's love. Thou wert once part of my very bowels; not so easily shalt thou now be torn from me.

To another he quotes from Isaiah: "Can a woman forget her infant, so as not to have pity on the son of her womb? and if she should forget, yet will I not forget thee". In one sad case his friends had evidently tried to comfort him; he had liberated his soul; he was clean from the blood of the sinner; but Bernard repudiated all such consolation. Most touching of all is an episode which is told in the *Exordium Magnum*, the earliest collection of Cistercian anecdotes.

On one occasion, he had been absent longer than usual for causes concerning the Church; for at the Pope's bidding, however unwillingly, he was oftentimes compelled to go forth for making peace, for healing some schism, or for confuting heresies. So, having unravelled that complexity of causes which had called him forth, he came back to Clairvaux, and entered the novice-room as soon as opportunity offered, in order that these his new-born tender children, whom he fed with his milk, might be the more copiously refreshed from the breasts of his consolation in proportion as they had long lacked the sweetness of his holy exhortations. Whithersoever the holy Father went, he sowed God's word over all waters, and scarcely ever returned without usury of spiritual gain, filling the Cell of Probation with a multitude of novices whose number sometimes reached the hundred. . . .

When therefore, as aforesaid, he had entered this Cell, and his persuasive and edifying tongue had cheered them all to the more fervent observance of their holy purpose, he called one aside and said unto him, "My dearest son, whence cometh this sadness which feedeth so fatally upon thy heart's core?" The novice scarce dared speak for shame. Then said this truly mild and humble man, who knew how to show himself to all men as a shepherd and no hireling: "I know, beloved son, I know how it is with thee; wherefore I pity thee with all a father's compassion and love. For during this my long-drawn absence, wherein perforce I lacked that bodily presence of my brethren which I so fervently desire, and God's grace supplied to my spirit that sight which my bodily eye lacked, then I was wont to return hither in soul, and to wander from room to room in diligent scrutiny of the demeanour of my brethren. In these wanderings I came unto this cell, where I found all the rest rejoicing in the fear of the Lord and girding their loins to the labours of penitence; but I sighed to see thee alone pining in bitter sadness. Then, when I would have caressed thee and drawn thee to myself, thou wouldst turn aside with averted face, weeping so bitterly that my very cowl was drenched with thy tears". With these words, and with the spiritual counsel wherewith the holy Father plied this captive soul, he put his grief to flight, and, from those depths of melancholy wherein he was almost overwhelmed, recalled him to the liberty of spiritual joy.

Here, then, is the real answer to those who see

in Bernard only the persecutor of Abailard; the former's superiority in character was even greater than the latter's intellectual superiority. Both men saw plainly enough what was at stake in this conflict of principle; it was the whole question which is now being fought out between Ultramontanism and Modernism. The final concession of Bernard's principle would have meant that, whatever reserves might be made by nobler minds, the majority would necessarily gravitate to Manning's contention that Authority is the one guide of the Christian conscience, and that the appeal even to historical facts is a treason and a heresy. Abailard, on the other hand, though his personal unorthodoxy has often been much exaggerated, would doubtless have been willing to go to all lengths rather than surrender his reason; and this application of reason to faith has gradually evolved doctrines entirely incompatible with the authoritarian position. And, here already in the twelfth century, the two champions were stamped each with the marked characteristics of his own school. Catholicism—to use the word in that widest sense in which it applies not only to the Roman but to a considerable party in the Anglican communion—has always shown more cohesion and a stronger social sense than its opponents, and has thus gone far to redeem its intellectual shortcomings. When individualism degenerates into selfishness, no amount of abstract truth will save it; the world is not so much moved by logic as by *savoir-vivre*; and the very wildest revivalist appeals more to humanity than the student whose speculations leave his own heart cold. Not that Abailard was lacking in feeling, any more than Bernard lacked intellect; but Bernard's combination of qualities was of a rarer type. True, he was as incapable of doing justice to Abailard's intellectual position as Bishop Wilberforce was of understanding the true significance of Darwinism; and, realizing how great an issue was at stake, he pursued Abailard unrelentingly so long as he judged him to be dangerous. But let us remember that, rare as those minds are which venture to pursue abstract truth to the very end—rarer still, those who, having found the truth, are fired with missionary zeal and willing, if need be, to go to the stake for the truth—yet rarest of all are those whose passion for souls is as absorbing as that other man's passion for knowledge; those who are willing to wrestle to the last, and, if need be, even to die at the last, for the men whom they see daily around them, with their common daily faults and unloveliness. Equal for equal, the love of speculation will never compete successfully with the love of our plain fellow-man. "Da mihi animas", as Dupanloup loved to quote in his missionary zeal; "da mihi animas; caetera tolle tibi".[1]

And it is this *vivace carità* which alone can explain Bernard's most extraordinary influence. Like some other saints, he had great power over dumb animals. When he came back from Italy in 1135, it was not only his own brethren of Clairvaux who felt that God's power was with them again, but

there flocked down, to meet him, from their rocky Alps, shepherds and cowherds and all manner of country-folk, crying from afar to seek his blessing; then they crept back up the mountain gorges to their flocks, talking together and rejoicing that they had seen the man of God, and that his hand had been stretched over them for the blessing which they desired.

We may compare this with what Cardinal Jacques de Vitry records.

For the prayer of innocents is most acceptable to God. Wherefore we read of St Bernard that, when he rode abroad in the morning and saw boys keeping their flocks in the fields, he would say to his monks: "Let us salute these boys, that they may answer to bless us; and thus, armed with the prayers of the innocent, we shall be able to ride on with an easy mind".

Popes, cardinals and princes gave way to him:

[1] Genesis xiv, 21. The A.V. and the Douay Version have "give me the *persons*" where the Vulgate runs literally "give me the *souls*".

"they say" (wrote his old pupil Eugenius III) "that it is you who are pope, and not I". Peter the Venerable and other distinguished churchmen were sometimes wounded at his unsparing words, but never irreconcilably. His letters and sermons,

Fig. 3. Shepherd of about 1200.

even over this distance of time, have the force of Newman's; essential simplicity, searching penetration into men's hearts through the preacher's knowledge of his own, and enough real classical culture to give uncommon clearness and freshness to the words which gushed from this deep and

27

living source. But the real secret was in the source itself: "Did not our hearts burn within us?" wrote one of his disciples in later years, feeling that nothing less than those sacred Emmaus-words could give a full measure of the truth. Bernard's eloquence was irresistible; mothers hid their sons, wives their husbands, to withdraw them from his compelling voice and glance. For this, moreover, we have the evidence of Giraldus Cambrensis, who was no blind admirer of the saint. He writes:

Another example is that of the blessed Bernard, who, preaching in French to Germans who were utterly ignorant of that tongue, stung them to such devotion and compunction that, with the greatest ease, he softened their hard hearts to the shedding of tears from their eyes, and to doing or believing all that he urged upon them; yet, these men had been altogether unmoved by the interpreters who faithfully rendered his sermon in their own tongue.

Think of the qualities which, in ordinary life, make for success without friction. One man sees his final purpose so clearly, and is so evidently concentrated upon it—menace and cajolery are so obviously wasted upon him—that the world finds it cheaper to let him have his own way. Another is so straightforward, so accustomed all his life to think aloud, that we pardon him the most inconvenient frankness; it is his way. A third is so unspotted from the world that we are forced to doubt of our own ideal where it clashes with his; another so loving and lovable that we have scarcely the heart even to correct his faults. St Bernard combined all these qualities, and more. Perhaps no such hard fighter ever made so few permanent enemies, especially since his common-sense marked clearly the limits to successful fighting. "When only one is angry," he said, "something may still be done; when both wax angry, there is no further profit." He made, then, an extraordinary number of converts, and kept them with extraordinary constancy to their new life. And to what a new life! No less than the original Benedictine Rule, in that strictness which had almost been forgotten through this lapse of centuries; and not only in all its strictness, but in something more; for, as we have seen, some tinge of exaggeration, however involuntary, must always colour the resolute reformer.

CHAPTER II

CLAIRVAUX

LET us look now into the abbey of Clairvaux, such as Bernard made it. In proportion as it was truly Benedictine, it contrasted in many ways with what the reader will be prepared to expect, and still more with the average medieval monastery, as revealed to us in intimate chronicles and episcopal visitations.

If we are to accept the numbers given in the *Exordium Magnum*—and these, however startling, are rendered credible by unimpeachable statistics as to the rapid increase of the Order—there were enough monks at Clairvaux to fill more than a dozen of the largest English abbeys. There were sometimes, we are told, from 700 to 800, in spite of constant drafts to other houses; and among these were from 80 to 100 novices. The puritanism was as strict there as at Cîteaux under St Stephen Harding; the church was bare; but in that same proportion the services were sung in spirit and in truth. There was no throng of layfolk in the nave; only the double choir of monks and lay-brethren; something of the plainness of early Clairvaux may be seen in the still-surviving abbey church of Fontenay, which was a daughter of Clairvaux and

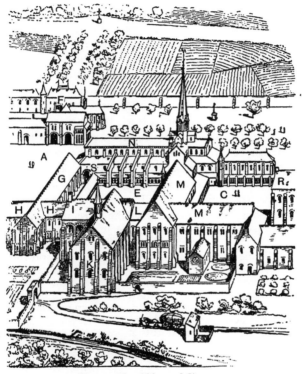

Fig. 4. The Abbey of Cîteaux.

A, Outer Court; **C**, Smaller Cloister; **E**, Main Cloister; **F**, Main
Gate; **G**, **H**, **H**, Lay Brethren's Quarters; **I**, Kitchen; **L**, Cale-
factory or Warming House (with Refectory, or Frater, between);
M, **M**, Dormitory (Dorter), with Chapter House underneath;
N, Church; **R**, Infirmary; **S**, Lay Brethren's Door. The Cistercians
were notable (1) for the number of *lay-brethren* and (2) for placing
their Refectories *at right angles* to the S. alley of the cloister.

31

dates from St Bernard's own lifetime. The life
there exemplified Newman's words: "The season
is chill and dark, and the breath of the morning is
damp, and worshippers are few; but all this be-
fits those who are by profession penitents and
mourners, watchers and pilgrims". "Sinner that
I am, my duty is not to teach but to mourn", so
wrote St Bernard, borrowing a sentence of Jerome's
which echoed all down the monastic centuries.
Here, then, the Cistercian lived from day to day
in silence, labour and prayer, "eating his own sins
and those of the world". For these monastic inter-
cessions were credited with the most miraculous
efficacy. We are told that

> While King Philip-Augustus was at sea, on the
> way to his crusade, there arose one night a violent
> tempest. The king asked his companions every
> moment what time it might be. When at last he
> learned that it was midnight, he began to comfort
> all the rest, sailors and travellers, saying, "You
> cannot perish; for at this moment thousands of
> monks are rising from their beds and will soon
> be praying for us; after whom the parish priests
> will soon arise also and give us their prayers. Then
> the monks will sing their masses, and then again
> the parish priests; wherefore it cannot be but that
> we are saved".

The storm did indeed abate, and men attributed
it to this clear proof of faith. The same story is

told of our Richard I, with special application to the Cistercians.

The Cistercian, mourning for sin, showed his inward compunction in outer severity. "Let the monk", writes Arnulf of Boyers about 1150 A.D., in that *Mirror of Monks* sometimes attributed to St Bernard; "let the monk have no familiar friend.... Let him be as Melchizedek, without father, without mother, without descent....Let him think as if he alone existed in this universe—only he and God." Music, held St Bernard, should be good but plain, and such as never to distract our attention from the words. He disapproved of poetry since his conversion; and indeed it was one of the clauses of the *Carta Caritatis*, the Foundation Deed, that no Cistercian should compose verse. When Bernard wrote the office for St Victor's day, at the request of the Victorines of Paris, the hymns were purposely so composed that they would not scan, though they lent themselves to chanting. Of him, as of St Francis, his biographer notes that he never laughed but by constraint; and he himself wrote to his former pupil, Pope Eugenius:

Jests [*nugae*] are but jests among worldly folk; in a priest's mouth they are blasphemies. It may sometimes be thy duty to bear with them if they befal thee, but never to repeat them....It is base to be moved to open laughter [*ad cachinnum*] and baser to move another thereunto.

Labour, too, had now again become a stern reality. One of the miraculous graces conferred on Bernard was in this field. He was distressed

Fig. 5. A Reaper (*c.* 1250).

that his bodily weakness prevented his reaping with the rest in harvest; he prayed for strength sufficient unto that task, and it was granted for the occasion. It was of this same bodily weakness that many of his sermons were born; that was his only way of sharing the general labour of the convent.

Next to his letters, these sermons do most to reveal his character; and of Clairvaux conventual life they tell us even more than the letters. Only fifteen sermons a year were prescribed to the abbot; but Bernard preached as often as he could find occasion. In the form in which we have these discourses, they were doubtless written down by the brethren with the help of the preacher's notes. A few exist also in French; it was once thought that these were delivered to the lay-brethren; but it is now generally admitted that they are almost contemporary translations from the Latin sermons. Some were delivered in the morning; for he breaks off at the hour of Mass, or else for that field-labour which, in the few critical days of harvest, superseded Mass. Others were evidently in the evening, for he speaks of nightfall, and of guests arriving who demand the brethren's care. Indeed, the concluding sentences of several of St Bernard's sermons on the Canticle cast upon him and his hearers those undesigned cross-lights which are so precious in what they add to, or discount from, the formal biographies of a saint. The sermons themselves are among the most striking productions of medieval mysticism, in their whole-hearted acceptation of this Oriental love-song, this Song of Solomon, as a story of Christ and the soul. "Let him kiss me with the kiss of his mouth; for thy breasts are better than wine....Stay me up with flowers, compass me about with apples, because I languish with love"; the first fifty-one of St Bernard's sermons will show us how these amorous outcries may suffer a sea-change from earth to heaven. This single verse supplies a text for eight of his sermons in succession. But the cares of earth constantly called preachers and hearers, even at Clairvaux, down from the Holy Mount. Guests come suddenly, and:

Brethren, it is good for us to be here, but lo! this evil day calleth us away....I will go forth unto the guests, lest anything be found lacking in that love whereof I am even now discoursing unto you; lest perchance it be said of us also "for they say, and do not".

Elsewhere, he complains still more pathetically of the impossibility of finding unbroken quiet for meditation. And he recognizes also the natural limitations of Brother Body. He has appealed passionately to his brethren: Can they trust in themselves alone, and work out unaided their own salvation?

Ye have done well to signify by that grunt [*grunniendo*] that this is not in your sense; nay, that ye are not so senseless, and that I need not labour so clear a point. But follow closely this next point.

36

Or should I not rather pause here, for the sake of those who are drowsy among you? I had thought to expound in one single sermon that matter of Twofold Ignorance whereof I had promised to discourse; and I would have done so, were it not that this seemed too prolix unto those who are hard to please; for indeed I see some yawning, and some already asleep. No wonder; they are excused by the vigils of last night, which were most protracted. What shall I say, however, unto those who slept last night, and who sleep none the less now? But I will not farther prick them to shame; let it suffice to have touched the spot; methinks they will watch better in future, fearing to be branded with our observation.

To listen in silence to a preacher was not a medieval convention; in the sermons of Berthold of Regensburg and St Bernardino of Siena we sometimes find a whole running fire of interruptions from the hearers and rejoinders from the preacher. In two other places St Bernard deals with similar expressions of feeling. Expounding a difficult passage of Origen, he suddenly breaks off: "What meaneth this unwonted *grunnitus*, or who among you is murmuring vague disapproval?" And elsewhere, after pressing upon them a high ideal of brotherly love: "Wherefore have some of your faces fallen at these words? For your deep groans betray your sadness of soul and dejection of conscience". For sleep at sermon we have evidence from Caesarius of Heisterbach, in the third generation of Cistercianism: "Many, especially of the lay brethren, were asleep, and some were snoring....I myself was present at that sermon [of Abbot Gerard]".

There we touch the human side of what, at its greatest, was an almost superhuman effort to create a new world. And we shall least err if we take it at its greatest, and attempt to comprehend these men's real aim. Let us try, then, to look into that chapter-house, dim in its own dusk (for even the church itself had only five oil lamps to light it) and dimmer still through the mists of nearly eight centuries. Let us try to feel for a moment as those hearers might have felt, and to realize that this was truly a venture of faith for all. One of the worst vices of what may be called the plaster-saint school of history—a fault almost as fatal as its inveterate temptation to tamper with documents—is that of rendering these very human men so unreal to us that we can scarcely profit by their example. Yet men of every creed, looking back, ought to hail these stern and patient reformers as victors in a great fight, however we may judge of the actual cause for which they fought. The meanest of them, as a rule, did something real, and something difficult, to overcome his own lower nature; yet even the best of them could not be absolutely assured of final victory. The most successful monk, except so far as he chose to deceive himself, felt the reality of St Paul's "lest that by any means, when I have preached to others, I myself should be a castaway". The religious sentimentality which would persuade us to regard the victory of these canonized saints as a foregone conclusion, is as false and as foolish as the patriotism which preaches that we can never lose a war. Minstrels are very much at their ease (St Francis reminded his disciples) when they chant the deeds of Roland and Oliver; but the doing of those deeds was a far harder and more dangerous task.

Caesarius of Heisterbach, in the third and fourth generations of Cistercianism, gives a long and motley list of the causes of conversion; but, even from the records of the first generation, we may see that conversions were already varied enough. There were men who had suffered a great moral shock, like that thief whom St Bernard begged from Thibaut of Champagne on his way to the gallows, promising that he would subject the man to a harder penance than hanging. There was the courtier who, in a vision, had seen his dead prince writhing in hell; there was the student who had the same ghastly ocular assurance with regard to his great teacher in the Schools. Most men had crept into Clairvaux out of the cold; chilled to the

39

very marrow with the conviction of the world's
wickedness and unfaith, and envisaging the cloister
as the only certain refuge; here, side by side, they
could keep each other warm in faith. Outside,
even within the Catholic fold, "rottenness and
corruption spreads in these days of ours through-
out the whole body...the wound [of the Church]
is inward and incurable". Grosseteste will say
practically the same, or stronger still, before the
Council of Lyons in 1245; two centuries later, the
greatest churchman of his century will echo it
again: "The church is wasted with an incurable
cancer, and the remedies do but make her worse".
Who can be safe in a world like this? and what
wise man can fail to see that the only prudent
speculation is to quit it once for all? Conversion,
therefore, is prudence. But there were others, we
must remember, who had not chosen the cloister
merely as the end of such a process of exhaustive
induction. Some had possessed a plenitude of love
and power, yet these things had not palled upon
them; possessing and enjoying still, they might
have gone on unsated to the very end; but here
in Clairvaux they recognized an even subtler
beauty, a more compelling power; and here they
fixed their deliberate choice: "This is my rest for
ever, here will I dwell"; *haec requies mea in saeculum
saeculi*. It was like the gospel-net, bringing in

small and great. If we ourselves, we of today, had come within that influence, some at least would have been caught in; those, perhaps, who would least have expected it and of whom it could least have been expected. Henry of France was a spoilt child of fortune; though as yet only a subdeacon, he held an archdeaconry and four great abbacies, for he was son to the reigning king. He came to St Bernard on worldly business, with an able business-man in his train, Andrew the clerk; once at Clairvaux, it seemed worth while to look round the abbey and commend himself to the prayers of the brethren.

The holy Father, among other words of exhortation, said unto him: "I am confident that thou wilt not die in thy present state, but that thou shalt soon find by thine own experience how great is the profit from those prayers for which thou hast asked". To the amazement of many men, this was fulfilled that same day, and the whole convent was filled with joy at the conversion of this young prince. Meanwhile, his companions and his whole train lamented as though they saw him dead; and, above all, a certain Andrew of Paris cried aloud upon Henry as drunken or mad, sparing neither insult nor blasphemy. Henry, for his part, besought the Man of God to labour more especially for Andrew's conversion. The Saint, in the hearing of many, made answer: "Leave the man to himself; his mind is now in bitterness; yet be not greatly solicitous on his account, for he is thine". Then

Henry conceived a greater hope, and was urgent that he should speak unto Andrew; but the Saint said, looking more severely upon the prince: "What is this? Have I not already said that he is thine?" Andrew hearing this (for he also stood by), being a very obstinate man and filled with loathing for our holy conversation, thought thus silently within himself, as he telleth even to this day: "Now I know thee hereby to be a false prophet; henceforward I will not spare to cast this in thy teeth before the King and his princes and in full congregation, that thy falsehood may be known to all men". Yet how wonderful is God in His counsels, above the sons of men, laughing at their vain struggles, and fulfilling His own purpose when and how He will! Next day, Andrew rode away, invoking every curse upon that Clairvaux wherein he left his lord, and wishing that the valley itself might be swallowed up whole with all that dwelt therein. Nay, those who had heard the Saint's words concerning him were no little moved and astonished when they saw him depart in this spirit. But God did not suffer their weakness and their little faith to be long put to the proof. For Andrew rode forth that one day, fighting as it were against God's grace; but, when night came, conquered and as it were bound in chains [*victus et quasi vinctus*] by the violence of that Holy Ghost who drew him, he could not wait for the day, but, rising before dawn, and hastening back to Clairvaux, he showed us a second Saul—or, rather, a second Paul—in his conversion.

Within a few months of this event, we find

Eugenius III writing to Louis VII: "Thy brother Henry, sprung from so ancient a line of kings, has taken the cowl and washes the dishes at Clairvaux". The next story of this same collection, telling how Bernard dispersed the gloom that hung over the saintly Geoffroi de Péronne at his first conversion, is almost equally striking.

There were many, of course, with whom Bernard himself failed; but a more solemn atmosphere of impending judgement was felt to hang about these cases. The monk was always tempted to magnify the sin of retractation in a novice, or to make mere infirmity into sin; but a novice who had fallen away from St Bernard was felt to have done direct violence to the Holy Spirit of God: still more, one who had actually put his hand to the plough. William of St-Thierry tells us of two such, and of one's latter end.

I saw him afterwards in the world, a vagabond and a fugitive from the face of the Lord like unto Cain; a man of great humility, so far as I could see, and miserable in his confusion, but too faint of heart. Yet in his last days he came back to Clairvaux, under compulsion of poverty and infirmity; a man of noble birth, but cast forth by all his kinsfolk and acquaintance. There he renounced his property, yet not altogether his self-will; and he died, not as a brother within that home, but at the gates, praying for mercy as a poor mendicant.

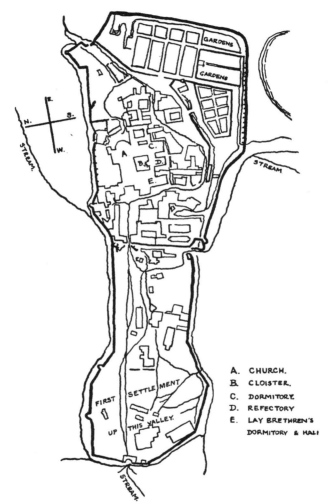

Fig. 6. Plan of Clairvaux as completed.

But backslidings in an actual monk of Clairvaux, even such partial backslidings as this, were almost unheard of. There was only one really striking exception, St Bernard's secretary Nicholas. The chroniclers could truly boast of their brethren that, numerous as they were and divers as their paths had been, when once they were settled in Clairvaux "the multitude of them were of one mind and one heart". Doubtless St Bernard's keen eye was on them from the very first; in all soundly-conducted novice-rooms, the difficulties of the Rule were not only plainly exposed but even exaggerated, for a full test of resolution and constancy: doubtless therefore many slipped out, and a few were quietly eliminated, before the time came for the final vow. But that vow, once taken, was kept in earnest. St Bernard showed scant sympathy with those who hoped to jog quietly onward to salvation; "far from me" (he protests) "be those who say 'we will not be better than our fathers'". With him, they must not settle down but go on from strength to strength, however difficult the progress may be; for "it is far easier to find many layfolk converted to good, than to find one monk passing from good to better". Therefore Bernard never sank into the difficulties which beset even so great a man as Samson of St Edmundsbury; indeed, it is most instructive to

compare an average well-conducted house, such as
Jocelin of Brakelonde reveals to us, with the missionary fervour which reigned in the first Cistercian
generation. Samson (his intimate Jocelin tells us)
was wont to groan on his couch for the trouble
that he had with his subordinates; and the cares
of office blanched his hair to snow. The monks
of St Edmund were respectable; but they hated,
with the bitter hatred of mediocrity, whatever
was more than respectable; it repented them to
have helped to choose a really great man for their
ruler. One brother would say: "May the Lord
Almighty give us a foolish and unlearned person
for our [next] abbot, that he may be compelled to
lean on us for help!" another: "Mine own counsel
will be, if I live [to see another vacancy], that we
choose some one who is no very good monk, no
very wise clerk; nor, on the other hand, one too
unlearned or too dissolute". Samson was evidently
in the minority at Bury; even Jocelin practically
confesses that he himself would have been content
with a less efficient abbot. But of Bernard it is
equally evident that he carried the overwhelming
majority with him at Clairvaux. What made this
possible, was his own compelling love; Dante's
"love, that compels love in return"; *amor, che a
nullo amato amar perdona*. His worst trials were in
his frequent absences from his brethren, from these

46

children whom God had given him. His letters are full of this.

> If ye suffer from my absence, think how I must suffer; for ye lack only my single presence, but I lack you all....My longing on my pilgrimage is to see the holy temple of God, which ye are....My little ones are weaned before the time; I am not suffered to bring up those babes whom I brought to birth in the Gospel.

He fulfilled, more truly than any other Benedictine of whom we have record, that precept from the second chapter of St Benedict's Rule:

> The Abbot ought always to suit his deeds to the greatness of his name; for he is held to take Christ's place in the monastery, when he is called by His name, as St Paul saith: *You have received the Spirit of adoption of sons, whereby we cry: Abba, Father.*

Those who had known him could thenceforward describe their religious conviction in concrete terms: "that which we have seen with our eyes, and our hands have handled". The path might be narrow and steep; but "to whom shall we go?" Clairvaux was their home not only from necessity but from passionate daily choice; *haec requies mea in saeculum saeculi*; and among the most pathetic touches in the early records are the indications of what we may call this *nostalgia Claravallensis*.

Hundreds went forth to found fresh houses; but all, if they could, would fain have died at Clairvaux. An old knight, Henry of Coutances, had been sent out with others to a colony in Normandy; after a while he felt his forces failing, and prayed for recall, that he might be buried in his spiritual home, in this Burgundian cloister where he had taken his first vows. Bernard's brother Guy, who himself had been a knight, was then "provisor", or steward, of Clairvaux. He refused to transport the old man on the score of expense; and St Bernard, when he heard of the incident, spoke his indignation plainly.

Hast thou more care for our money or our beasts than for thy brethren? Seeing therefore that thou wouldst not suffer our brethren to rest by our side in this valley, thou thyself also shalt find thy last rest elsewhere.

So Guy died at Pontigny, far from that valley which in old days had been called *The Valley of Wormwood*, which Bernard had humanized and civilized, and which even today, in spite of later associations, has lost none of that mingled beauty of forest and tilled field. To Bernard himself, this house was what the Portiuncula was to St Francis; and he writes in one of his letters: "My prayer to God is, that mine eyes may be closed by the hands of my children, and that my poor body may be laid at Clairvaux side by side with the bodies of the poor".

For, here, all his human affections were interwoven with his higher faith. Few men doubted, in his day, that monachism was above all others the heavenly way. The common word for a monastic Order was *Religio*, and the ordinary sense of *Conversio*, even in Canon Law, was "taking the monastic vows"; it may safely be said that medieval writers use it half a dozen times in this sense for once that they use it in Wesley's sense. And although Bernard, like most good men, may have shrunk from any temptation to regard his own salvation as assured, yet he had no doubts for all his brethren who remained loyal to the spirit of their conversion. He shows no trace, I believe, of the gross but very widespread superstition which regarded the frock and cowl as an all but impenetrable armour against Satan; his confidence was based on the belief that monastic life was the true Gospel life, the real narrow way.

You ask me about brother Guerricus [a recent convert]. He so runneth, not as at an uncertainty; so fighteth he, not as one beating the air; nevertheless, knowing well that it is neither of him that fighteth nor of him that runneth, but of God that showeth mercy, he beseecheth thy prayers on his behalf, that He who hath already given him grace to fight and run, may grant also that he may conquer and attain.

If Bernard sometimes expresses that "assurance of personal salvation" which Newman somewhere speaks of as characteristic of post-medieval puritanism, it is because he had a good conscience and a truly filial trust in God. "The elect...is initiated, and is carried forward; shall he despair only of the consummation of his bliss?" And again, writing to a nun, he bids her answer the scoffs of worldlings with Pauline confidence: "My glory is hid with Christ in God; and when Christ, my life, shall appear, then shall I also appear with Him in glory". "Let no man who now loves [God] disbelieve that he himself is beloved...we hold a double proof of our salvation." And his confidence is increased by the sense of new life in this new Order; he swims on the rising tide of the Cistercian reform. "It is indeed as though that tree, whereon the Lord of Glory hung, had now shot forth new buds....It is He Himself who gathers you, as the most precious fruit of His cross." It was in this intimate alliance of spiritual exaltation with active life that St Bernard, and others with him, found their real liberation from the formalized demonology of the Middle Ages. On the one hand, they would never deny, and sometimes they would even consider with involuntary horror, the pains of hell, the nearness of hell to all men, and the actual dominion of hell over the unredeemed multitude. But they deliberately fixed their gaze, as the good men of all ages have done, rather upwards than downwards. These horrors (they would have said) are undeniable; but what matters to us is, that we have a power of putting them under our feet—a choice, a freedom of the will, by which most men live instinctively even when they argue against it. Bernard's thoughts, therefore, are concentrated not on the awful contingencies which speculation might reveal, but on the felt sense of sonship to God, and of a possible reward far beyond his deserts. He is keenly conscious of the Pauline and Augustinian antithesis, of the greatness and the littleness of man; but it is on our greatness that he will dwell, and, by contemplation, help to realize that which he contemplates.

Soul of man, whence hast thou this? Whence hast thou this inestimable glory, that thou hast earned the place of spouse to Him on whom the angels desire to look?...What shall I render unto the Lord, for all the things that he hath rendered to me?

But the most striking act of Bernard's faith is recounted in one of his early biographies. A monk of Clairvaux, unable to believe in the Real Presence, had yet enough faith to be convinced that he would be damned for unbelief. St Bernard's attitude was uncompromising: "What! a monk of mine go down to hell? God forbid!" Then, to the poor doubter himself,

he said not: "Hence, heretic!—begone, thou damned soul!—away with thee, lost wretch!"— but commanded boldly: "Go and take the Holy Communion with *my* faith!"...The monk, therefore, constrained by the virtue of obedience, though (as to himself it seemed) utterly without faith, came before the altar and communicated; whereupon, being straightway enlightened by the Holy Father's merit, he received a faith in the Sacraments which he kept unspotted even to the day of his death.

Such, then, was Bernard's audience at these sermons; such was his attitude towards them; and his themes were in natural harmony with that mutual relation. To questions of conduct he applies the exactest rule of reason; on strictly religious topics he speaks the language of exhortation or of mystic contemplation. His most elaborate homilies —that course of sermons on the Canticle which was interrupted by his death—though they contain some of his directest satire, deal mainly with mystic exposition; the story is that of Christ and His Bride the Church, or of the excellence of Mary. The Rose of Sharon, the Tower of Ivory, the Garden Enclosed—*hortus inclusus*—recur and recur with those mystic implications whose haunting memories Renan describes from his own seminary days. But a great part of the sermons is strictly practical, as from an abbot to his spiritual children, for whose souls he must some day render a strict and solemn account. One theme is the evil world; evil even in the Church of Christ; the city, with all its boasted civilization, is a mere prison; the cloister is your only heaven on earth. Yet the cloister is but what we ourselves make of it; no vow will save us the labour of working out our own salvation; if, under the cowl, we do not bear the true monastic heart, then we are of all men most miserable.

Such men labour with Christ, but with Christ they shall not reign; they follow Him in His poverty, yet they shall not be with Him in His glory; they drink of the brook by the way, but shall never lift up their heads in heaven; they mourn now, yet shall they not be comforted.

The way is rough; but we must look for no relief from creature-comforts.

Thou pleadest..."cheese burdens my stomach; milk gives me a headache; my chest suffereth not that I drink mere water; cabbages foster melancholy and leeks breed bile; fishes from a pond or muddy stream are utterly unprofitable to a man of my complexion". Here, brother, is no question of thy complexion, but of thy profession; thou art not a physician, but a monk.

Worse still must be our spiritual trials; it is the good man, above all others, whom Satan tempts in the form of an angel of light; the Virgin Mary herself had reason to suspect, for a while, lest the divine message might have been one of these glorious but fatal lies; this is the *daemonium meridianum*, the Tempter disguised as an Angel of Light, who sometimes deceives even the elect. And this our fight, bodily and spiritual, is life-long; your abbot, like his master Christ, tolerates no shirking of responsibility. "Can a Christian, before the hour of his death, cast off the obedience once laid upon him? Was not Christ our Master made obedient to his Father unto the death?" There was felt to be a sacramental significance in one of Bernard's acted parables, when he came into the novice-room at meal-time, followed by a lay-brother bearing a great basket filled with slices of cheese, from which the abbot gave to each of the novices, saying as he distributed them: "Eat now, brother, for thou hast a long way yet before thee". Neither there nor at any other time did he disguise the difficulties, but his faith trod them down; *plures cum nobis*; "they that be with us are more than they that be with them": the mountain is full of horses and chariots of fire round about us.

Nor did he disguise his own temptations and weaknesses. "Oftentimes, in the early days of my conversion, my heart was dried up and withered within me"; it was frozen, and the spring tarried long; "more and more it languished, and weariness came upon me, and my soul slept in weariness, sad almost to despair, and murmuring to itself: *Who shall stand before the face of His cold?*" He was long haunted by the face of a girl upon whom he had gazed too long and fondly before his conversion. As his own physical strength decreased, the burden of his care for others grew heavier and heavier: he besought them to spare him, yet was forced, in the next breath, to retract that cry of self-defence,

lest one of the weaker brethren, in his fear of troubling me, should dissemble his own needs beyond his powers of endurance....I will not use my privilege of retiring into myself; rather, let them use me as they will, so only that they come to salvation.

His work left him no moment of freedom; yet in work was his remedy; work, even when it took him away from Mass, or when manual labour called him away from his book. He frankly recognized the dignity even of worldly business; let the monk, entrenched in his spiritual fortress, do full justice to those secular clergy who risk their souls outside in grappling with the world's work. He exacted the utmost from others and from himself; until, as we have seen, he found himself reduced to the last humiliation of eating delicacies in the infirmary by command of his superior abbot of Cîteaux.

This, perhaps, is the most pathetic of all the stories told about the saint; it is far more significant than the derogatory tales recorded by Walter Map, who intensely disliked the Cistercians. However much importance we may attach to Map's evidence, and however we may emphasize other weaknesses which for proportion's sake, and therefore for the sake of general truth, I have not dwelt upon in this necessarily brief sketch of Bernard the monk, the final picture must be that of a man of rare virtue and distinction, whose devotion will be honestly admired by those who least share his religious ideal. And, if his body broke down under the unfair strain which he laid upon it, this in itself is among the noblest of infirmities. Can any man justly blame the ascetic but those (if those there be) who have tried such self-subjugation, and stopped short at the exact point at which protest came no longer from the body but from the spirit? The world will always respect the scars of self-denial as it respects those of the soldier; and few men have had a better right than Bernard to plead St Paul's words: "Henceforth let no man trouble me; for I bear in my body the marks of the Lord Jesus".

CHAPTER III

THE CISTERCIAN IDEAL

IF, however, personal criticism of St Bernard is
disarmed by his sufferings, and by his unre-
mitting thought for others down to his last
sickness, yet this should not forbid our criticism
of his ideal. On the contrary, the greater our ad-
miration for his person, the more inevitably we
turn to compare his life-story with the history of
his foundation—for he may truly be reckoned as
the main founder of Cistercianism. Why could not
this greatest of all Benedictines bring the generality
of Benedictine society back to the real Rule?

The failure, in itself, is frankly confessed by contemporaries, and is disguised only by modern
apologists who ignore contemporary evidence.[1]
We may account for it partly by natural reaction;
Bernard, it may be said, demanded too much from
himself and from his brethren; he would have got
more if he had asked for less, and civilization would
have been better served. There is a certain amount
of truth in this, and it is recognized by medieval
monastic disciplinarians themselves, naturally as

[1] I have collected these contemporary criticisms in *Five
Centuries of Religion*, vol. II, chapters xxvi–xxvii and Ap-
pendixes 34–5.

they shrink from the farther conclusions which we ourselves may be tempted to draw. The author of the *Exordium Magnum* notes the difficulty of preventing each new generation of monks from starting on the lower plane of self-denial at which their predecessors, worn out by a life of asceticism, had finished. Again, he emphasizes the almost impossibility of calling a community back from relaxations once permitted; Cistercianism, like many other great and beneficent institutions, was actually founded on an inclined plane, and was therefore subject to a natural decline from century to century, in spite of occasional revivals. And St Bonaventura bears the same witness with regard to his brother-friars, when their founder was dead and their Order had become a great European institution. It would be inhuman, he says, not to permit considerable relaxations to the aged and broken-down friars; but then

they are no longer able to set an example as of old; and the young friars, who never saw their real work, imitate them only in what they now see in them, and become remiss, and spare their own bodies under the excuse of discretion, lest they should ruin their health as the old friars did.

The older friars fear to correct this, lest the younger should retort, "Your words are good enough, but your deeds do not bear them out".

Therefore, when these younger men come to rule in the Order, they bring up the next generation in their own likeness, so that the early friars are now become a laughing-stock, rather than a model for the rest.

"Le mieux est l'ennemi du bien": there was less discretion in Bernard than in Benedict, and therefore his work was less durable. But was St Benedict's own work, wonderfully as it stood the test of time, guided by perfect discretion?

"Time, the devourer of all things, deadeneth even monastic religion, since mankind is more prone to imitate vice than virtue." So wrote the chronicler of the *Exordium Magnum* in about 1200 A.D.; but we, while admitting his facts, shall hardly accept his explanation. One of the most decisive social gains since the Middle Ages is the gradual decline of that pessimism which saw little hope but in the speedy coming of Antichrist, and Armageddon, and the end of all created things. We believe in the gradual perfectibility of human nature; and, though our temptation may be to take this belief too easily, that is at least a nobler error than to make it a point of faith that man is more prone to vice than to virtue. If monachism in general failed to satisfy the best minds even in 1200, and has since lost ground steadily with the large majority of thinking people, we must seek the causes of failure not in human nature, but in the nature of this institution which fails to satisfy the legitimate demands of humanity.

That is the key to the revival which we connect with the names of Francis and Dominic. If, a century after, it needed what some men account a greater than St Bernard to institute reforms which rather superseded than recalled true Benedictinism, then the fault was not in Bernard but in the system. Not but that the earlier monastic leaders, and the best of their followers, had shown as fine qualities as any that we can trace in history; but there was something in the ideal itself which the later Middle Ages were outgrowing. No doubt the inmost core of the Rule is suited to every age; we can scarcely conceive a society in which some few groups, here and there, might not find profit in this type of celibate common life, devoted to a high ideal and controlled in details by sound common-sense. But as a world-institution, richly endowed in lands and rents, and even richer in the prestige of its spiritual past, built upon the conservative instincts of an uneducated population which regarded monachism as an apostolic ordinance, coeval with and inseparable from the Christian church—as an institution of that kind, monachism was beginning to outlive its day; and not even those eight great revivals of 1020–1120 could save it from decadence.

What was mainly wrong with it was that tinge of "holy boorishness", *sancta rusticitas*, as St Jerome called it, which it had partly inherited from the anchorites of the desert, and partly been forced into by the corruption and turbulence of Western society in those centuries from which the monks took their character. Incidentally, the monk did a great deal of good in the world, even directly; but his primary object was, confessedly, to save his own soul by retiring from the world; we have seen this already, and shall see it again. Therefore men like St Bernard, overflowing with the milk of human kindness, had to force themselves to be less generally sociable than society would have desired of them. Bernard did, indeed, constantly mix with the outer world, but most reluctantly, and only because the world could not do without him. And to a little extent even in him—far more clearly, therefore, in inferior saints—we may trace this tendency to puritanical aloofness which was very strong indeed in certain quarters of the medieval Church, and especially among cloisterers of all Orders—for even the friars often fell back into it.[1] One remarkable dialogue is reported to have taken place between the late cardinals Manning and Vaughan. The latter, aristocratic by birth

[1] See the 4th of my *Medieval Studies: The High Ancestry of Puritanism*.

and imposing in manner, remarked once with just a tinge of religious superiority: "The natural man in me has no love of the world". To which Manning instantly retorted: "So God loved the world, that He gave His only-begotten Son—". We must not thus array Bernard and Francis personally against each other; but we may fairly put the average monk here in Vaughan's place, and the average friar in Manning's.

As we need to understand the strict Benedictine ideal in order to realize how good a monk St Bernard was, so also we need to mark how closely St Bernard felt bound to follow the Rule, in order to understand that problem which Benedict had set to the Western Church, and which Bernard re-stated in all its original force. The essential points of this problem come out the more clearly, the better we bear in mind the latter saint's natural breadth of view, common-sense, charity, and sense of humour.

I have had occasion more than once to emphasize the puritanical side of medieval monasticism, and here, again, we must return to this subject, since it lends itself, perhaps, to more misconceptions than almost any other. A modern author of repute can even write: "The monk, it must be remembered, was in no sense 'a gloomy person'....In fact, the true Religious was told to try and possess 'angelica hilaritas cum monastica simplicitas'". The monastic moralist of the Middle Ages would have repudiated the sentiment of this first clause as vehemently as he would have rejected the Latinity of the second. Modern apologists are fatally hypnotized by the monastic life of the present day; and their strangest mis-statements are often due not to perversity, but to an ignorance which is serenely ignorant of itself, and which even the critical outsider can fathom only at the expense of much laborious verification of references. There is no corner of Christendom where the present church buildings are so inartistic, in general, as in Tyrol and Southern Italy, though they have been in uninterrupted Catholic occupation since the days when Catholic art was at its highest level. Similarly, on many points of medieval history, none are so complacently blind as those who can boast an outward continuity of tenure, and who therefore regard the past uncritically through their modern ecclesiastical spectacles, dispensing themselves from documentary research because they trust in the living oracle at their door. The truth is that the very vitality of Catholic traditions, so far as they are still vital, has constantly shown itself in change. The Tyrolese and Italian churches have been held by generation after generation of worshippers, in whom the sense of present useful possession has

outweighed—and, on the whole, has justly outweighed—the antiquarian sense of responsibility
to a far-off past. Those buildings have been knocked
about and beplastered and Jesuitized, because the
Jesuits and their pupils for a while were the living
teachers in them. Thus, again, modern monasticism shows some real vitality in its frank neglect
of many among its most ancient traditions; and
the pressure of outer society has changed it even
more, perhaps, than any purely internal evolution.
Monks are very few now, scattered among not very
sympathetic populations; they live under a glare
of publicity and a pressure of public opinion not
only far more exacting than any in the Middle
Ages, but far more powerful to enforce actual
obedience upon those from whom it exacts it
theoretically. The modern monk lives under severe
religious competition; "by their fruits ye shall
know them"; he cannot afford to answer this test
less successfully than Anglican or Wesleyan,
Christian Scientist or Agnostic. Thus, the pressure
of outside opinion relieves the strain on many of
the disciplinary clauses of the Rule. St Benedict,
for instance, instituted something like strict vege-
tarianism as a moral safeguard; the modern monk
can be trusted by his superiors to eat meat like
other people. Again, he no longer even pretends
to labour in the field like his predecessors; and so

it is with many other early provisions which, side by side with their modern modifications, are alluded to in chapter xviii of Abbot Butler's *Benedictine Monachism*. And not only is the modern monk thus more sheltered by social laws than his ancestor, but he is better sifted by natural selection. In the days when warfare was not occasional but chronic —with constant private warfare even at times of international peace—when a saint like Bernard could say even of his own Church that "her wound is inward and incurable"—thousands of men and women pressed indiscriminately into the cloister as their only possible refuge. Thither (quite apart from the motley crowd of unreal converts to which Caesarius of Heisterbach introduces us) came men who found the world too hard, and who sickened of the intolerable choice between slavery and rebellion: they steered for an ideal haven, as an Italian of the Risorgimento put it, "where there are neither slaves on the one hand, nor rebels on the other"; *dove non son nè schiavi, nè risorti.* Thither came ladies (for the lower classes, as a rule, had no such commodious refuge) who were liable to be bought and sold with their lands; who in their own houses could not secure what we now consider the decencies of civilized life, but were subject to brutalities not only in thought and speech but in deed; who, again, outside their homes, were too often dependent for the sacraments of the Church upon a priest with whom no self-respecting woman could be seen talking alone. Many more, both men and women, came in by no choice of their own, but by parental compulsion. Among these ill-assorted communities, even the *tria substantialia* of Poverty, Obedience and Chastity could be maintained only by strict attention to minor precepts; on that point medieval disciplinarians are untiring, emphatic and unanimous; and St Bernard would not have been more incapable of forecasting a world given over to Protestantism, than of anticipating an age of monasticism in which the *tria substantialia* no longer needed the regular and immemorial safeguards of labour and abstinence from meat, claustration and moneylessness and silence. The only monk with whom Bernard had to deal lived in a far harder world than ours; without were fightings, within were fears. Monasticism was what St Benedict had called it, a warfare; the monk must strike hard, and it was not easy to do so with a smiling face; in the scores of surviving medieval disciplinarian treatises, the model monk is a puritan. Even Francis never laughed outright; to Bernard, as we have seen, monastic merriment was what Dr Johnson would have called "mighty offensive": *foede in cachinnum moveris, foedius moves.* We have seen how Bernard loved to echo from

Jerome "the monk's business is not to teach but to mourn"; *monachi non docentis sed plangentis est officium*; the cloisterer helps his brother-man not directly but by his ascetic example. Bernard's *angelica hilaritas* differed not in nature and perhaps not even in degree from the serenity of all men who, through very different outward expressions of faith, have reached a deep inward calm. With Baxter or Bunyan, John Newton or Jonathan Edwards, we can imagine an intimate friend recording some such flash of splendid sunlight as we find in the casual words of one who visited Bernard in his mean cell at Clairvaux,

like unto a leper's hut at the crossways....And when he in his turn had welcomed us joyously, and we began to ask how he fared, he smiled upon us with that generous smile of his, and said "Most excellently"—*modo illo suo generoso arridens nobis: "Optime", inquit.*

There we have the peace of God that passeth all understanding, worthy of reverence wheresoever we meet with it, but not confined to any single creed. The time is long past for supporting any form of Christianity on a foundation of historical disguise; it was already past even when Newman wrote. Feeling that some men might resent, in 1873, his republication of historical studies written in his Anglican days, he added a word of justification in his Preface:

> Nor is this the sole consideration, on which an author may be justified in the use of frankness, after the manner of Scripture, in speaking of the Saints; for their lingering imperfections surely make us love them more, without leading us to reverence them less, and act as a relief to the discouragement and despondency which may come over those who, in the midst of much error and sin, are striving to imitate them;—according to the saying of St Gregory on a graver occasion, "Plus nobis Thomæ infidelitas ad fidem, quam fides credentium discipulorum profuit".[1]

A learned and very honourable theologian of our own day remarked once, after reading a volume of historical criticism which tended too much towards iconoclasm: "That book has shattered my ideal". So Jerome wrote when Alaric had sacked the Eternal City: "When Rome perishes, who is safe?" But with Jerome this was a passing weakness; and to Augustine the fall of Rome pointed the way towards greater eternities. The earthly city may perish; "Babylon the Great is fallen, is fallen"; but the Heavenly City is imperishable; the unseen good shall, in the long run, triumph over the too obvious evil; there remaineth a sabbath-rest for the people of God. That book of

[1] "The unbelief of Thomas has helped us more to our faith, than did the faith of those disciples who believed."

Augustine's was perhaps the earliest philosophy of history, as it still remains, in essence, the truest. Our noblest energies are not numbed, but stimulated, by even the coldest truth; the atheist Leopardi was as momentarily untrue to his best self as Jerome was when he gave way beneath the shock of unwelcome facts.[1] If we can no longer believe that our ideal has been, we may at least reply that it shall be; it may not have been our actual starting-point, but at least it shall be our goal; there remaineth therefore a sabbath-rest for the people of God.

For Benedictinism, as for his own person, St Bernard would no more resent fair criticism now than he feared it in his lifetime. If he had been born with us, there is much in modern life which he would most heartily have welcomed. He would have had scant sympathy with the attempt to prejudge deep religious questions by superficial appeals to sentimentality or to artistic preferences. The principles on which he adopted and defended monachism were very different from those on which we are often asked nowadays to regret the Dissolution of the Monasteries. The empty rhetoric and sentimentality which fills a book like Mr Ralph

[1] "E, con la vista impura, L'infausta verità" (*Risorgimento*). Compare De Musset's sonnet: "J'ai perdu la force et la vie, etc."

Adam Cram's *Ruined Abbeys of Great Britain* would have been as abhorrent to him, in its own way, as even Abailard's doctrines were. To realize this, it is only necessary to read his *Letter to Abbot Guillaume de St-Thierry*.[1] Brother Giles, one of St Francis's closest disciples, boldly rebuked a fellow-friar who complained of unjust banishment: "Who can banish a friar, whose home is always in heaven?" St Bernard, in the same spirit, would have repudiated the essential irreligion of those who ask us to condemn the religious revolution of the sixteenth century because it destroyed even more medieval art, perhaps, than has been destroyed among orthodox populations by Jesuit and rococo rebuilders. Splendid churches were as alien to Benedict's ideal as to that of any other great religious reformer; and Bernard was in deadly earnest to bring monachism back to the Benedictine ideal. Therefore, as many over-enthusiastic Mary-worshippers of the later Middle Ages were tempted to undervalue this man who had written against the Feast of the Conception, so the modern romantic medievalist is often less than just to a reformer who, as they plainly hint, showed a definite taint of puritanical Pharisaism. For the romanticist,

[1] This is unfortunately among those not translated by Eales. The pertinent portions of this are translated on pp. 169 ff. of my *Life in the Middle Ages*, vol. IV.

the ideal cloisterer is to be found less among the Cistercians than in the monk of Cluny, with his greater dignity and *savoir-vivre*, and his wider services to art. For, though Cluny itself had begun in great simplicity, yet it soon blossomed out into a great artistic school; and, beautiful as Cistercian art also became, this was always due rather to the layman who worked on the church than to the General Chapter of Cîteaux itself, which strove from generation to generation, until the cause had become too evidently hopeless, to maintain the puritanic plainness prescribed by the first founders.[1]

[1] For Cistercian art, see M. Lucien Bégule's admirable monograph, *L'Abbaye de Fontenay* (Paris, Laurens, about 3 f.), also E. Sharpe, *Cistercian Architecture* (1874), and J. Bilson in *Journal Royal Arch. Inst.* vol. 66 (1909). It is only in a certain sense, however, that we can speak of a Cistercian school of art; so far as this Order shows separate characteristics these are due to the influence of conscious restraint and simplicity upon the ordinary Burgundian school of Gothic architecture. Enlart puts it admirably: St Bernard insisted on the puritanical side, but the contrary impulse was too strong, and "de cette doctrine excessive il ne resta qu'une certaine simplicité de bon goût que l'on pourrait considérer comme un raffinement de plus" (*Manuel d'Archéologie française*, I, 1902, 202).

CHAPTER IV

PRECURSORS OF ST FRANCIS

AT the turn of the twelfth century into the thirteenth, we are in a period of considerable unrest, both inside and outside the monastery. Within, it is still possible for the majority to "sit far in the interior, wrapt in their warm flannels and delusions, inaccessible to all voice of Fact"; but, without, the world is drifting away from the cloister. The peasant had often some real excuse for anticlericalism, and even for irreligion; more and more he felt and resented his abasement, by contrast with the citizen, who himself had but recently struggled up from bondage, and whom Church lords, as well as lay lords, were sometimes attempting to enslave again. And here, as often, freethought flourished, especially at the two extremes of the social scale. Rough lords often disbelieved because they hated Church discipline; quick-witted scholars at the universities, because they had read the Arabian translators and commentators of Aristotle; they now knew too much to accept certain factors in the current teaching, and passed on to reject the whole. The peasant, at the other end, often knew too little, and was too heavy-witted to think or feel as the Church required him. Men of all classes frequently felt that the institutional Church was not really doing the best work that might be fairly expected of it, just as they felt a century ago about our great Public Schools. There were some whom she evidently did not satisfy, for even the strictest Cistercian or Premonstratensian, poorer than the peasant individually, was collectively rich, and this is why the Cistercian General Chapter was scandalized at the abbot who, in 1180, attempted to raise money for rebuilding a devastated abbey by sending monks to beg round the neighbourhood. Other "possessionate" monks had done this, but the early Cistercians did not care to do it. Yet often, before the Cistercians, there had been individual monks who revolted against the "possessionate" system, and lived for a while, at least, by begging. Molesme itself, from which Cîteaux grew, began in what practically amounted to mendicancy. Again, in 1092, we have the "five poor clerks" whose association finally grew into the abbey of St-Martin-de-Tournai, and who "had nothing to live upon; but certain religious layfolk carried sacks daily round the town and cried aloud for help for these Poor Men of St Martin; they lived thus for a year from hand to mouth". Shortly afterwards, when a noble woman begged for admission into Religion, the abbot made her prove her vocation by begging

and working for her livelihood. A generation
later, St Bernard of Tiron anticipated St Francis
in his begging, as also in his conversion of a wolf,
and in his use of that word of extreme surrender
"naked, to follow the naked Christ", which comes
already in St Jerome's epistles (no. 125) and was
also claimed by St Bernard of Clairvaux. There are,
indeed, many natural anticipations of St Francis
in St Bernard's writings. His description of his
friend St Malachy (§ 43) reads like a chapter from
the *Fioretti*; this man who was always cheerful yet
never laughed; this bishop who refused to possess
bondmen and bondwomen and farms, or any endowment whatsoever, not even a house of his own.
Or, again, that passage from Bernard's third
Nativity Sermon (§ 5), where he takes his text
from the rich snoring on their feather beds in
complete ignorance of that Christmas revelation
which was made to the poor shepherds: "let men
learn, therefore, that they who labour not with
their fellows deserve not to be visited by angels".
And it is not merely jealousy of a rival Order which
inspires the author of the Dominican *Vitae Fratrum*
to claim the Virgin Mary's preference for "those
brethren upon whom there pressed, for man's
salvation, heavier labours than those which lie
upon other Religious who save their own souls
individually—*qui se singulariter salvant*—labours

heavier, but more fruitful, and filled with ineffable joy".

For the world of 1200 was broadening fast, and it is the distinction of that age that the laity themselves were beginning to show an example of Christian revival, not only individually but collectively. The nobility were shaken by the Crusades, by the subdivision of fiefs, and by personal extravagance. Those same crusades, and the dispersion of noble fiefs, had given a proportionate upward impetus to the towns, especially on the main trade routes. In southern France and northern Italy, much of the ancient Roman civilization had survived, and men were comparatively educated; the classics were read to some extent. Here, then, freethought and heresy were passing from the sporadic to the endemic stage. Toulouse and other great towns of Languedoc, by the evidence of orthodox writers of the time, had been anti-Catholic almost from time immemorial; generation after generation was being born into heresy. But, side by side with this, there were three great movements which started in orthodoxy, drifting only later into revolt by much the same process which turned the later Wesleyans from Churchmen into Nonconformists. These three movements were those of the Waldensians, the Humiliati and the Joachites. In tracing what these men strove to be, we shall see more clearly what the average monk had ceased to be, and what the friar had not yet arisen to become.

Peter Waldo was a rich merchant of Lyons, the essential purity of whose purpose shines forth even in the pages of the anonymous Premonstratensian of Laon, and of Étienne de Bourbon, that strict Dominican who laboured so hard to destroy the Waldensian sect. The former gives a detailed account of Waldo's conversion under the year 1173. He writes:

This man had heaped together much money by the iniquity of usury. One Sunday he turned aside to join the crowd which he saw around a *joculator*, and was so pricked to the heart by the man's recital that he took him to his own house and hung intently upon his words. Now that passage in the man's story told how St Alexis met his happy end in the house of his father. Next morning Waldo hastened to the school of theology, in order to enquire for the good of his soul; and, having been told many ways of coming to God, he asked the master which might be the most certain and perfect way of all. The master laid before him that sentence of our Lord: "If thou wilt be perfect, go and sell all that thou hast", etc. Then, going to his wife, Waldo gave her the choice of keeping what she would, either his movables or his real property, lands and waterways, woods and meadows, houses, rents, vineyards, mills and ovens. She, albeit with much sorrow, being compelled to make a choice, fell upon the real property. Then Waldo, from his movables, restored all that he had unjustly won, and gave a great part of his money to his two daughters, whom he had made nuns of the order of Fontevraud without their mother's knowledge; then he spent the greater part of his money upon the poor.

The next stage of his conversion is told by Étienne de Bourbon, who writes of the Waldensian sect:

These men are also called "Poor men of Lyons", because they there began their profession of poverty. But they call themselves "The Poor in Spirit", because the Lord said "Blessed are the poor in spirit"; but these men are truly poor in spirit, poor in spiritual goods and in the Holy Ghost. Now this sect began thus, as I have heard from many men who saw its founders, and from the priest Bernard Ydros, who was very rich and honoured in the city of Lyons, and a great friend of the Dominicans. This priest, when he was young, being a scribe, was hired by the aforesaid Waldo to write the first books in French which the sect possessed, at the dictation of a certain grammarian named Étienne d'Anse, who made the translation. This Étienne I have often seen; he was afterwards a canon of the cathedral of Lyons, where, falling from the upper chamber of a house which he was building, he met with sudden death. A certain rich man of this city, named Waldo, hearing the gospels [at Mass], and not being very familiar with Latin, was curious to understand their meaning. Wherefore he covenanted with the said priests, that one should translate into French and the other should write at his dictation, which they did; thence he did the like with many books of the

77

Bible and with many authorities of the saints arranged under heads, which they called *sentences*. These the aforesaid citizen read oftentimes and learned by heart, until he purposed within himself to keep evangelic poverty after the example of the apostles; wherefore, selling all his goods in contempt of the world, he cast his money into the mud unto the poor, and presumed to usurp the office of the apostles, preaching about the streets and places of the city these gospels and the rest which he had learned by heart, assembling many men and women to follow his example, and teaching them the gospels. These he sent also to preach through the villages around, people of all the lowest occupations. These then, men and women, unlearned and ignorant of Latin, scouring the villages and creeping into houses and preaching in the public places and even in the churches, provoked others to follow their example.

The rest of the story is only what we might expect from the circumstances of that time. The preaching of these illiterate men generated scandal; the archbishop forbade it, but Waldo and his friends, in 1179, appealed to the pope. He granted their petition on condition that the preacher, in each case, should obtain leave from the parish priest; a reservation which none will blame under the circumstances, but which was certain to cause friction. The movement, growing with extraordinary rapidity, was soon out of hand; in 1184 it was condemned by the pope, and these Waldenses or

Vaudois, solemnly as they protested their own orthodoxy, were driven out of the Church as John Wesley was driven in later years. Continuing to multiply with great rapidity, they were often forced into alliance with other heretics, but they still lived on in the mountainous districts to which inquisitors could hardly penetrate; thus Milton's Vaudois and the Vaudois of today are their descendants. Their main significance to us is their Bible-thirst; from this time forward the issue is clear-cut between a section of the laity sincerely anxious for full leave to learn and preach the story of Christ's words and deeds, and a clergy no less sincerely convinced that such a permission, since it must encourage private interpretation, could only end in the ruin of souls. I have printed, in the 7th of my *Medieval Studies*, Étienne de Bourbon's acknowledgement of the accurate Bible-knowledge possessed by these Waldensians. Monks and parish clergy had not been wont to give the Gospels to the people, nor even to preach the Gospel in the full sense. At the average parish service no sermon was heard, and the first general movement towards systematic popular instruction and preaching ended now in heresy. Yet it had begun in the Spirit, and in real promise. We have the evidence of another unsympathetic, but able and observant contemporary, the famous archdeacon Walter Map, who was himself in Rome when the Waldensian deputation came to Alexander III. "These men", writes Map, "have no fixed abode, and go about two by two, barefooted and without linen under-garments, without possessions, holding all in common as the Apostles did, following naked in the footsteps of the naked Christ." Thus far, we have what might be a description of St Francis and his companions, trudging to Rome past the walls of great cities and castles and abbeys, intent only on that which had absorbed Jerome's and Bernard's soul:

And to the lord Pope they presented a book written in French, wherein were the text and [authorized] gloss of the Psalter and of many books both of the Old and of the New Testament. These men besought with much earnestness that they might be confirmed in authority to preach; for they thought themselves experienced, whereas they were scarce beginners.

The pope told Walter to test them:

I began, therefore, by putting to them the easiest questions, whereof no man ought to be ignorant, (knowing that an ass, when he has thistles to munch, makes little account of a lettuce), "Do ye believe in God the Father?" They answered, "We believe". "And in the Son?" "We believe." "And in the Holy Ghost?" "We believe." Again, "in the Mother of Christ?" And they, again, "We believe". So all present mocked them with shouts of derision, and they departed in confusion.

Popes and prelates, in a critical mood, might well laugh this down, but it may be doubted whether the average country priest and his congregation would have avoided the pitfall. Here, for instance, is the Latin couplet with which a university sermon began at Oxford in the fifteenth century, and which is printed by Dr Owst on p. 318 of his *Preaching and Preachers in the Middle Ages*:

> Per consueta suffragia pulsentur mente pia
> Pater, proles deifica, spiramen cum maria.

"Let [these] be importuned with pious mind through the accustomed prayers; the Father, the Divine Son, the Spirit, with Mary." However, whether we sympathize with the simpletons or with the archdeacon, we may see plainly how the incident foreshadows an inevitable breach between the Waldensians and the hierarchy.

The Humiliati of Milan came to a similar end, though their origins were different. According to the story generally accepted until recently, they began under high Church patronage, and St Bernard gave them a Rule in 1135. But the latest research seems to prove that their first foundation was on what the Church regards as a heretical basis. Zanoni holds that

their origin must be sought in the struggle of the

Italian proletariat against the rich *mercatores*, and in that general state of unrest through which this country passed in the eleventh century. Not being able to create a trade-union under civil law, they formed a religious league which grouped the starving workmen and their families; they organized themselves in a gild with religious, economic, and social aims. That breath of revolt against the Church which agitated the sects passed also over the Humiliati; the Cathari or Patarini of Milan came partly under their influence, and part broke off to form the autonomous group of *Poor Lombards*, which for some time was fairly closely connected with the Waldenses. One group remained faithful to the Roman Church, and to the commands of Lucius III and Innocent III. The latter gave them a Rule, borrowed partly from St Benedict's, partly from St Augustine's.

Gradually this Order developed a threefold division: (1) semi-monastic brethren and sisters, analogous to the well-known Beghards and Béguines; (2) a lay group, answering to the Tertiaries of St Francis and St Dominic, and finally (3) a clerical branch for ecclesiastical services. The first two groups worked in combination, mainly at weaving; "originally, they fought against the ring of *negotiatores* who were introducing into Italy the fine woollen stuffs of England and Flanders". The contemporary Premonstratensian of Laon thus described them: "They live a religious life at home in their own families, abstain from lying, swearing and lawsuits, go simply clad, and champion the Catholic faith". But in 1179 the pope forbade their preaching in public; the Laon chronicler tells us that they disobeyed and allowed themselves to fall under excommunication. Thenceforward they allied themselves with the Waldenses, with whom they were expressly condemned in 1184; it was only a fraction to which Innocent III gave the Rule in 1201. These orthodox Humiliati, though they lasted on until after 1560, were always far less numerous than their rivals, the Waldenses, the Beghards and Béguines, and (later) the Tertiaries of the Friars.

All these movements point to a violent, though often vague and scarcely articulate, social and religious ferment among the multitude. As men grew more civilized, as the trader and artisan began to swamp the feudal element, it was natural that they should struggle for an open Bible and for liberty of preaching, and that they should implicitly condemn monachism as too self-centred and too far aloof from the multitudes that needed salvation. The Middle Ages had never forgotten that sane criticism of St Jerome upon "a holy boorishness which profited itself alone"—*sancta rusticitas solum sibi prodest*. And the third, perhaps the most important, of these pre-Franciscan movements came from a monk of one of the strictest

83   6-2

Orders, whose experience had gradually convinced him that the world needed not so much new forms as a new spirit. "The Calabrian abbot Joachim, endowed with prophetic spirit", to whom Dante gives so high a place in his *Paradiso*, was born on the confines, and literally within sight, of three civilizations. From his native mountains he could see the hills of Greece, where Christianity often ran apart from the Roman channels, and of Sicily, where Jew and Mohammedan worshipped and philosophized under a rule of tolerance. Joachim himself, if we may believe his somewhat romantic pupil and biographer, spent a memorable part of his youth in Constantinople, where he saw the horrors of a great plague, and in Syria, where he visited the holy places, made friends with Saracens, and enjoyed their reciprocal charity when he caught a fever, the children bringing him fruit and cheering his convalescence with their prattle. After a solitary Lententide upon Tabor, the Mount of the Transfiguration, there came to his cavern a vision "on that night when Christ rose victor over hell", which inspired all his later meditations and writings. Leaving Tabor, he followed from place to place in Christ's footsteps, seeking everywhere to heal the spiritual and moral sores of the people, but forced at last, like his Master, to weep as he looked down upon the land that he was quitting, in prescience of the calamities to which it was doomed. We next find him a Cistercian in Italy—first, as simple lay-brother, then, quite irregularly, as volunteer mission-preacher, and finally as prior and abbot of Corazzo, for which his noble birth and learning naturally marked him. He had long resisted the call to the abbacy, and now he found the business duties of his office an intolerable hindrance to his Bible-study and contemplation. A personal appeal to Pope Lucius III brought him exemption from the rule of *stabilitas loci*, and licensed him to dwell in any Cistercian house. He wrote most of his books as a guest in the abbey of Casamari. In 1190 we find him talking at Messina with our King Richard, who was attracted by his fame as a prophet; in 1192 he was in a hermitage, and the Cistercian General Chapter summoned him to appear before them, under pain of condemnation for contumacy and apostasy; but his licence to study where he chose had meanwhile been confirmed by Urban III and Clement III. He now founded a reformed branch of Cistercians in Calabria, building Fiore as the head abbey of the group, and for this he procured Celestine III's approval in 1196. In 1200, he informally submitted his writings, so far as they were completed, to the judgement of Innocent III, adding that, if he died before completing them and procuring their formal ratification, his brethren must correct them and submit them to the Holy See, for "I am ever prepared to observe that which the Papal chair hath decreed or shall decree, and never to defend any opinion of my own against its holy faith". His presentiment was justified: in 1202 he died without having procured any formal ratification; his Everlasting Gospel remained the unauthorized vision of a solitary seer.

This Everlasting Gospel was not the title of a book, but represented Joachim's conception of the spirit of the future, based upon Rev. xiv, 6: "I saw another angel flying through the midst of heaven, having the Everlasting Gospel to preach unto them that sit upon the earth, and over every nation and tribe and tongue, and people". As Christ preached the first Gospel, so Joachim now conceived himself to be announcing the final evangelical message. His ideas show how, from his youth onwards, he had lived and thought under the spell of the East—the spell of religious daydreams. Between Latin and Eastern thought there has always been a wide difference, even in Christianity. The East always conceived the Faith, to some extent at least, as a subject of discussion; the West, dominated by the Roman conception of law, has always regarded it rather as a deposit to be kept intact—*stare super antiquas vias*. God, the

Universal Lawgiver, has issued a code which may perhaps need continual refinement of interpretation, but which is essentially unchanging and unchangeable. From this static conception Joachim did much to free himself. Whereas it would be difficult to find any previous Church reformer of his standing who had not conceived his own reforms as a return to the past, Joachim frankly looks forward to an entirely new future. He dreams of a Church not static but organic; his theory is a Theory of Development. The world's history falls into three ages, of which the first lasted 1260 years, from Adam to Christ—the Reign of the Father.[1] The second, the Reign of the Son, shall last 1260 years also; let us remember that Joachim was writing up to 1200 A.D. and died two years later. In 1260 or thereabouts—our author wisely leaves a margin for error—shall come the Reign of the Holy Ghost. The first was the Age of the Old Testament, the second of the New Testament, the third shall be that of the Eternal Gospel—no new book, but a gospel proceeding from the Old and New Testaments, read with purer and clearer

[1] It is remarkable that the Bábí creed attached the same mystic importance to this period of 1260 years; see Prof. E. G. Browne's *New History of the Báb*, 1893, p. 288. Was this an ancient idea latent in Muslim thought, to be picked up separately by Joachim in the twelfth century, and by Mírzá 'Alí Muhammad in the nineteenth?

eyes: "For the letter killeth, but the Spirit giveth life". The first age was of the married state, the second of the priesthood, the third shall be *par excellence* the age of monachism. Yet it will differ from the monachism of the past, transcending it as the Eternal Gospel overtowers past conceptions of the Bible; these monks of the Third Age will supersede the secular clergy, but will themselves mostly lead the life of the primitive hermits, wrapt in contemplation of the Holy Scriptures. We look in vain for clearer detail; Joachim naturally shrank from too great precision. Enough for him and for his followers was the overmastering conviction that, within the measurable future, a golden age should realize what past ages had vainly striven for, and that the miseries of this world of 1200 marked only the darkest hour before the dawn. In that new world, men should see the truth no longer through a glass darkly, but face to face. Not that this was to be an age of rationalism—far otherwise; it was to be a time of mystic contemplation and mystic intuition, nourished by prayer and psalmody. Psalmody will inspire them to find in their Bibles the Everlasting Gospel. Led not by reason, but by the Holy Ghost, they will have no less freedom than the freethinker; each will follow his own inner light as confidently as any man can follow his reason, for "where the

Spirit of the Lord is, there is liberty". And this liberty shall far exceed the merely relative liberty of the Second Age; for, whereas that is the Age of Faith, this Third shall be the Age of Love. Unheard-of calamities shall herald it; bloodshed beyond any bloodshed of the past; only the Elect shall survive; and this chosen remnant will form the society of the New World. Such men will have risen above the love of riches; they will not merely passively accept poverty, but positively welcome it, remembering the poverty of Christ. Joachim, who in his own reformed monastery seems to have made no attempt to dispense with corporate possessions, appears clearly to anticipate a stricter poverty in the coming age: "it shall be like unto the age of the Apostles, when men did not acquire earthly possessions or inheritance, but rather sold them". Another oft-quoted saying of his does not really anticipate anything beyond the personal poverty of the true Benedictine, yet in another way it already suggests St Francis: "He who is a true monk, reckons nothing to be his own but his lute". Joachim's Model Religious anticipates the "God's Minstrel" of Franciscanism; his soul is attuned to the Holy Spirit not by meditation only, but by music also; not only by the Psalms, but by psalmody.

The Third Age, therefore, will be governed by

a sort of holy communism, by a natural and instinctive Liberty, Equality and Fraternity. Whether this is to reign among all men, or only among those Religious who set their seal upon the period, Joachim leaves undetermined. Or rather, we may probably answer for him: if all the world is to live this strictest monastic life in hermitages, then the first generation of the Third Age will also be the last. But we must not press him too far; his vision is abundantly fulfilled if we assume for this Age of the Holy Ghost a predominance of good equivalent to the predominance of evil in the Italy of his time. Let wars now become as exceptional as peace had hitherto been; let money-grabbing become abnormal, and contented poverty the normal condition; let the vast majority of the clergy live truly after their profession, and only an exceptional minority give cause for scandal; herein we should have already a sufficient Reign of the Holy Ghost; an age which, after long groaning and travailing in pain, would have burst forth into the glorious liberty of the children of God.

Joachim's personal loyalty was unquestioned, but here was a most revolutionary theory, explosive as all living thought must be in a society which is stiffening more and more into formalism.[1]

[1] "The thirteenth century believed that it had realized a state of stable equilibrium, and...their extraordinary

Remarkable from any point of view, his speculations are most remarkable, perhaps, in their escape from official condemnation after his death, and in the negative, if not positive encouragement which they seem to have received from three popes during his life. The fact is, that the medieval Church admitted far more licence of thought than has been possible since the Council of Trent, provided always that such freethought was not too plainly formulated and did not become too popular. The hierarchy, like every other human system of government, was here guided mainly by opportunism. Nearly a century before Joachim, a storm was raised in Christendom by Abailard's presumption in applying rational methods to the study of theology; methods which were afterwards adopted by Peter Lombard and all the great schoolmen, and are those of Roman Catholic orthodoxy to this very day.[1] Again, a century after Joachim (1318), four friars were solemnly burned as heretics on several counts, one of which was that they

optimism led them to believe that they had arrived at a state close to perfection" (M. de Wulf, *Philosophy and Civilization in the Middle Ages*, 1922, p. 268). Prof. de Wulf here ignores, of course, the many critics and rebels; he is thinking only of the orthodox philosophers and the hierarchy.

[1] The essential rationalism of the scholastic method is admirably drawn out by Dean Inge in his essay on Newman (*Outspoken Essays*, 1920, p. 189).

refused to wear the pattern of frock commanded by their General, adhering to that meaner form which Francis had worn. Another was, that they would not go begging (as Francis would certainly not have begged) for goods to be laid up in the friary storehouses. Abailard, therefore, was condemned, even as these four strict adherents of St Francis were condemned, because the one's thought and the others' practice had become matters of public scandal, which threatened real danger to the authorities. Midway between them, uncondemned, stands this Joachim whose theories imply the gradual abolition of the Roman hierarchy, and almost (it may be said) of the whole sacramental system! He is not by any means the first medieval thinker to take an organic rather than a static view of the Church; even his theory of evolution is to some extent anticipated by Tertullian, and in Augustine's *City of God*. But he was the first to bring those speculations into far greater clearness and actuality, and to kindle men's minds —if only those of a limited group—to the idea of an evolution which implies (if we follow his words to their conclusion) an Origin of Species in Christianity. Tocco is inclined to trace this tendency to Manichaean influences imbibed partly from the Greeks. Greece did certainly influence him. He puts St John (whom he regards as the founder of the Greek Church) above St Peter; he emphasizes the greater diligence of the Greek clergy in Bible-study, and their stronger tendency towards the contemplative type; on only one capital point does he feel the West definitely superior—in its stricter legislation as to clerical celibacy. But his main theories would seem to owe far more to Islam, which essentially rests upon this idea of successive revelations, each complementing and to a great extent superseding its predecessor, and all culminating finally in the Prophet. Joachim certainly wrote far more freely in his own corner of Calabria, if he did not think more freely, than he could have done at the University of Paris. In his speculations, as in the spiritual struggles of Othloh of St Emmeram and a few other similar documents, we get a glimpse of the abysses which must often have yawned before the monastic mind. "In silence and in hope shall be thy strength"; that text brought supreme comfort to St Bernard. But in less balanced minds such enforced silence does not always engender hopes; weariness of soul and melancholy—*accedia*—are constantly specified among the worst trials of the cloister, and it needed a strong mind to insist unflinchingly upon the hope that lies beyond. The Waldenses and Humiliati show us a laity struggling for reality in religion, and trying to tread that narrow way which

93

the average monk had ceased to tread. Joachim shows us the higher monasticism, conscious of its past failures, and struggling to become once more the regenerator of human society. In his attitude towards the insufficiency of the then Benedictinism, as in his sympathy with the poor, he is a true forerunner, if not an actual teacher, of St Francis.

On the first of these subjects he writes explicitly in his *Exposition of the Apocalypse*, commenting upon Rev. iii, 4–7. There he tells us that there are many monasteries founded in the name of St Benedict,

wherein some chapters of the Rule are so abolished [*absorta*] as though the saint had never published them; I speak especially of manual labour, of abstinence in food and drink. It is well known that, wishing to become rich under the Rule of poverty, they have become delicate and tender, feeble and infirm, men who must be fed with milk and not with solid food. Nor need we wonder: for who, living among riches and delights, could ever lead a life of poverty, and keep his purpose of chastity among such abundance of food? Moreover, many [*pluraque*] monasteries are situated within cities and villages; here they find things at hand which entice the monks' minds, and (I grieve to say) which sometimes take them captive, put out their eyes, and lead them away to Gaza. I say nothing of the worst crimes, the stench and the cry whereof riseth even unto heaven....Why then hath this evil befallen the fifth Order[1] (which is prefigured in the Angel of the Church of Sardis), but for this reason, that they have not borne in mind what they have heard and their fathers have told them, how idleness is the enemy of the soul? If they be true monks, let them live by the labour of their hands; let all abstain from flesh-food, save only the sick and infirm; let two cooked dishes daily suffice to the Brethren. Nor, I say, for the infirmity of divers natures, let them be allowed the use of wine, which [as St Benedict saith] is not in truth a thing for monks—let us so use this (I say) as never to drink even to drunkenness and satiety— let the monks possess nothing of their own—let them remember that it is not expedient to dispute of the colour or texture of their garments...and that furs and linen garments lead them astray from the true monastic goal, especially considering our Lord's words: "Behold they that wear soft clothing are in kings' houses". These and like commands the Benedictine Order hath received from its father and leader; yet in some monasteries these are as utterly suppressed [*suffocata*] as though they had never been prescribed.

He goes on to expound how evil monks are prefigured in the Raven of Noah's Ark, good monks in the Dove, and he adds:

That there have been such doves in the monastic Order, yet few and far between, is shown in the next verse [of the Apocalypse], where it is added:

[1] In his scholastic division, the monks form the fifth Order of human society.

"Thou hast a few names even in Sardis who have not defiled their garments; and they shall walk with me in white robes; for they are worthy". Although therefore there are many in this fifth Order who knew not the time of their consolation, yet shall the Lord be consoled in his remnant, of whom it is written [as aforesaid]: "Thou hast a few names even in Sardis which have not defiled their garments".

It will be noted that, though he is evidently speaking mainly of the older Benedictines, he does not expressly exclude his own Cistercian Order, and Professor E. G. Gardner is probably right in supposing that it was this which finally brought him into conflict with the General Chapter.

Joachim writes of the poor in this same book:

For there are some rich folk, though very few, who have a great household of servants and hand-maidens and yet come to the Kingdom of Heaven, because they pity, even as a father pitieth his own children, these others over whose heads they are set in this world; and because they strive to treat these with the same compassion which they themselves hope to receive from God the Lord of all. But the rest do not thus; nay, if ever their inferiors, ground down by the burden of servitude, murmur against them, then, not considering how the Lord of all creation hath chosen these poor to be His especial friends, they meet a little word of complaint with grievous revilings, calling them wicked slaves and boors and perjured,...and with much confusion and fear they drive them forth from their presence. Therefore these humble folk themselves, when their time shall be come, shall cover with fear and confusion the face of Babylon, saying, "Lo is this that Babylon, that city of the proud, that of old oppressed the humble in her power? now is she become as it were the mire of the streets, and as the dung of the whole earth, full of all ignominy and perpetual confusion". Wherefore the elect will reward as it were double to this Babylon, reproaching her people with the miseries of their calamity. Nor shall they confound them only by returning like for like in setting before them their worldly injuries, but also by putting before their eyes the pains of Hell, to which that Babylon is condemned for ever.[1]

Whether St Francis took any direct stimulus from Joachim or not, this Calabrian prophet shows us what ideas were in the air. And his influence upon many of the early Franciscans is unquestionable; indeed, over one extreme though not inconsiderable section of the Order his influence became paramount, as we shall see. Meanwhile there were two points in his prophecies which impressed even moderate Franciscans with a conviction of actuality. The Raven of Noah's Ark, betokening the imperfect Religious, wore the colours of the Black Monks of St Benedict; the perfect Religious, the Grey Dove with its message

[1] We must not be shocked at this last sentence; it was one of the commonplaces of orthodox theology that the bliss of the saints in Heaven would be heightened by the sight of the torments of the damned: not, of course, directly, but only accidentally.

from God, must plainly prefigure the Grey Friar. Again, there was one blank place in Joachim's elaborate scheme, which inevitably whetted men's curiosity. To each of the First and Second Ages

Fig. 7. Benedictine and Cistercian.

he assigns a leading character. For the first it is naturally Abraham, for the second Jesus Christ, for the third no name is given. Moreover, these great figures had their heralds: Adam went before Abraham; Elijah and John the Baptist before

Christ. Of the Third Age, Benedict had been the John Baptist: but who was to be its Messiah? When, only a few years after these prophecies, St Francis appeared, was it not inevitable that his

Fig. 8. Franciscan and Peasant.

disciples should seize upon this vacant niche and appropriate it to their master? Benedict's day was waning and the dayspring of Francis was come: *quasi sol ex oriente* became a text dear to the new Order of Mendicants.

CHAPTER V

ST FRANCIS

THE Waldenses and their fellows testify to a popular movement, very immature in those days, which came to a crisis at the Reformation and is beating again at our gates today. Joachim, on the other hand, shows us the feeling of bankruptcy within the inner sanctuary of monachism, and the yearning for a new world. That new world came presently in a different form, by a change less catastrophic and universal than Joachim had expected, yet with startling and enduring force, under the leadership of Francis of Assisi, with whose name we must associate also that of the Spaniard Dominic. Different as these two men were in themselves, yet the two Orders soon came very close together by attraction and interaction. Franciscans and Dominicans worked so nearly for the same ends, and learned so much from each other, that they may conveniently be treated together. The Dominicans soon approximated very closely to Franciscan poverty, and the Franciscans to Dominican learning. Other Orders of friars, of which the Augustinians and Carmelites alone were permanently authorized by the papacy, followed closely on the lines of the first two. All four differed widely from the older Orders, and it was the Franciscan who showed this originality *par excellence*. St Bernard and St Francis are complementary; each helps us to understand the other.

Even the most unsympathetic student must ask himself at the outset why Francis succeeded so far in an enterprise in which Waldo and other precursors had failed; and the answer is supplied by such early and intimate documents as Thomas of Celano's two *Lives* of the saint; the *Speculum Perfectionis* and the *Tres Socii*, which represent (to what exact extent will probably always be disputed) the recollections of his closest companions; and the *Little Flowers*, which enshrine the traditions preserved among the peasants of those remote or mountainous regions where he had been most at home, and his memory was dearest. Of these four the *Mirror* is most valuable to those who can read between the lines; and its keynote is struck in the very first chapter, with which we must connect chaps. 41 and 68. This last tells us how, at the General Chapter of the Order held towards the end of St Francis's life, when the Order had grown so large as to be half out of hand,

very many wise and learned among the brethren went to the Cardinal of Ostia who was there,[1] and said unto him: "My lord, we will that thou

[1] Ugolino, whom the pope had deputed at Francis's request as Protector of the Order, and who afterwards became pope as Gregory IX.

shouldest persuade brother Francis to follow the advice of the wise brethren, and sometimes to follow their guidance". And they quoted the Rules of Saints Benedict, Augustine and Bernard, which teach men to live after such and such an Order. But when the Cardinal repeated all these things to the blessed Francis by way of admonition, then the blessed Francis made no answer, but took him to the brethren assembled in Chapter, to whom he thus spake in the fervour and force of the Holy Ghost: "My brethren, my brethren, the Lord called me by the way of simplicity and humility, and showed me this way of life in truth, for me and for others who will believe and imitate me. Wherefore I will not have you name unto me any [other] Rule, whether of St Benedict or of St Augustine or of St Bernard; nor any way and form of life except this which the Lord in His mercy hath shown and given unto me. And the Lord said unto me that He would have me a new covenant in this world, and He would not lead us by any other way than by this knowledge. But through your learning and wisdom God will confound you; and I trust in the sergeants of God,[1] that He by their hands will punish you, and that you will yet come back again to your first state, willingly or unwillingly, with shame to yourselves". Then the Cardinal was sore amazed and made no answer; and all the brethren were in great fear.[2]

[1] The devils, to whom God gave leave to punish sinners; cf. chs. 67 and 71.

[2] Sabatier, in his notes to this chapter, points out that "the *Conformitates* gives a remarkable variant: 'And the Lord hath told me that He wished me to be a great fool in this world'—*unum magnum fatuum in hoc mundo*".

With this passage, we may compare others which testify to Francis's repudiation of precedent, and his insistence on the saving grace of his own new Rule (chaps. 26, 78–81, 88). He dwells upon his right to originality: "The Lord would fain have one new and small people, unique in itself and different from all that have gone before". Francis will listen to no counsel of conformity with other ideas which he judges to be at least partly outworn; he reproaches those who "put before my people the example of the ancients, and make light of my exhortations". With all his humility, he was stoutly self-assertive where occasion seemed to require it; for, in asserting himself he was convinced that he asserted Christ. That, indeed, is the secret of his unique combination of originality and obedience. With all his repudiation of tradition, he was never disloyal in thought to the papacy. How far his ideas were essentially consistent with the papacy as it then was, or as it was ever likely to be, is a very different question, upon which scholars are likely long to differ. It may be contended that he sowed seed which, in its growth, was as fatally destined to burst merely static Roman Catholicism asunder as Christianity had been destined to disintegrate static Judaism. But of his loyal intentions, and of his pacific and persuasive methods, there can be no doubt; and, in ultimate analysis, we shall find that this is because the positive elements so immeasurably outweighed the negative in his mind. Most of us are tempted to assert the wrongness of others with far more confidence than we should feel if we were staking money on the rightness of our own ideas; with a few, it may be said that their whole creed is composed of such negatives, reducing itself to a catalogue of their differences with their fellow-men. No Christian ever had less of this than St Francis. Even where he most differed from his fellows in fact, he was least ready to mark the difference, so long as the men themselves were such as he could respect. He did the hardest thing in the world in the perpetual conviction that it was the easiest, and that all men, if they tried, would find it so; naked, he followed the naked Christ. And in the completeness of this surrender to Christ he found a perpetual harmony among all human differences; his life was hid with Christ in God; all other human souls rested actually or potentially in the same refuge; all human differences, except the eternal difference between good and evil, were merged in that essential oneness. His originality, including his unique combination of radicalism and obedience, sprang from the singleness of purpose with which he strove to become the exact follower of Christ.

Yet no saint was ever more human; it is one of M. Sabatier's great services to history that he has rendered from henceforth impossible the old conventional portrait of Francis in orthodox biography. There are many biographies of the saint now, of very unequal merit; but even the least critical of these volumes contrasts most favourably with the ordinary biography of 40 years ago. The *Mirror* shows him as "poor, despised, illiterate"; the doctor who attended him in later years realized his greatness only at that moment, and remarked to the brethren "neither you nor I appreciate this man's sanctity". The pious and enthusiastic missionary Jordan of Giano confessed, in after-life, that he had valued far too little the living Francis. The contemporary biographer Thomas of Celano says concerning him: "Saintlier than the saints, among sinners he was as one of themselves". No man in this western hemisphere ever succeeded in rendering himself more independent of outward things, not so much with ascetic aims as because he felt that to be the freëst, happiest, most real life. Here, again, his mind was not negative but positive; as Dr A. G. Little has written: "We are accustomed to think of a poor man as one who lacks riches; S. Francis thought of a rich man as one who lacked the inestimable boon of poverty". And certainly—though we must beware here of much random and exaggerated writing on the subject—his teaching and example did much to make honest poverty respectable.

That, then, is the first of the two main reforms which he brought into the old monachism. The Benedictine—even the Cistercian, and even Joachim's reformed Cistercians—had been individually poor, but collectively endowed. They themselves had confessed frequently enough that endowment might prove a fatal snare, but they had never yet ventured out into the cold. The Order of Grammont had come nearest to such a venture; but, after a generation or two, even they had become indistinguishable from the rest. Francis, who had for himself chosen absolute poverty long before founding any Order, clung strictly to the same ideal all through. Christ's apostles, he thought, had no common purse except for the poor: therefore we will have no common purse. And, apart from his imitation of Christ, he supported this by a business argument which strikingly anticipates Thomas Hodgkin's frank confession when he was pressed to declare himself on the question of defensive warfare. This Quaker leader wrote: "If war is absolutely condemned under all circumstances by the Sermon on the Mount, Business, as we understand it, is also condemned" (*Life*, ed. Louise Creighton, p. 240). And similarly: "If we should have possessions", said St Francis, "we should need arms to protect ourselves. For thence arise disputes and lawsuits, and for this cause the love of God and our neighbour is wont often to be hindered, wherefore we are minded to possess naught of worldly goods in this world". This was as courageous as it was logical, and Francis with his earlier companions lived up to their logical convictions. So long as they were only a small group, and could do so without dislocating the labour market, they lived from hand to mouth by manual labour, treating mendicity only as a second resort. St Francis writes in his *Testament*:

I worked with my hands, and I wish to work, and I wish firmly that all the other brothers should work at some labour which is compatible with honesty....And when the price of labour is not given to us, let us have recourse to the table of the Lord, begging alms from door to door.

But this was not to burden society; rather this lightened the social burden as few movements have ever done. Without marking the contrast explicitly, Francis fought with all his might against the two subtlest temptations of the older Orders— endowed idleness, and deadness of soul, the *accidia* of Chaucer's *Parson's Tale*. In the face of incurable sloth, even Francis's tolerance gave way: "Go

forth, brother Drone!" was his command to a friar
whose hearty appetite contrasted with his reluctance
to pray, work, or beg (*Mirror*, chap. 24). Nor would
he suffer cheerless faces among those who were
tramping to glory in his company (chap. 96).

For on a certain time he did rebuke one of the
companions who appeared sad of face, saying,
"Wherefore dost thou show outwardly the pain
and grief that thou hast for thine offences? Keep
this sadness between thyself and God, and pray
Him of His mercy to spare thee and to give thee
the gladness of His salvation, which thou hast lost
by the fault of thy sin. But before me and the rest
strive ever to be joyful; for it beseemeth not the
servant of God to show sadness and a dismal face
before his brethren or any other man".

Here was an early Christian virtue; even in St
Augustine's time the temper of the Christians,
"serena et non dissolute hilaris", was one of the
things which attracted him to the Church. Yet
we cannot quite understand St Francis and his
times unless we take note of brother Leo's next
sentence in the *Mirror*:

Not that we are to understand or believe that
our father, that lover of all soberness and decency,
would have had that joy shown forth in laughter,
or even in the least vain word; for this showeth
not spiritual joy, but rather vanity and folly. Nay,
rather he had a singular abhorrence of laughter or
idle words in God's servants, whom he would wish

to abstain not only from laughter, but also from giving to others the least occasion for laughter.

We may discount these words to some extent by reading into them the desire, which even Leo shows sometimes, of separating his hero from all human

Fig. 9. A Jongleur (*c.* 1250).

weaknesses. But, even so, we must see in Francis something of Bernard's mind; the highest Christian cheerfulness must stop short of actual laughter. In a few other ways, also, Francis betrayed something of the older monastic puritanism, into which the next Franciscan generation slid back still farther. He loved music even more than Bernard; he won men not only by song but even by secular song: his disciples were to be "God's Minstrels", and something more familiar still, for the word *joculator* connotes buffoonery quite as strongly as music. Yet for pictorial or plastic art, like Bernard, he cared nothing, holding that the poverty of Franciscan churches would do more for pure religion than the costliest elaboration of ornament. Like all great reformers, again, he was comparatively unsacerdotal. For the priest's person and office he prescribed the utmost reverence, but he contemplated only one Mass a day in his communities, and very few friars of the first generation were in holy orders. In spite of his frequent disapproval of extreme asceticism, he confessedly shortened his own life by ascetic austerities, and he sometimes showed an almost Manichaean contempt for Brother Body (chaps. 16, 61). Moreover, like all revivalists, he sometimes exchanged the gospel of love for a gospel of fear. There is vivid terror in his description of the death-bed of one who remembers his kinsfolk, but forgets the poor.[1]

[1] *Opuscula S. P. Francisci* (Quaracchi, 1904), p. 96. Compare General Booth's confession, "Nothing moves the people like the terrific. They must have hell-fire flashed before their faces, or they will not *move*".

Ye think long to possess the vanities of this world, but ye are deceived; for that day and hour will come whereof ye think not; which ye know not now, but ignore it. The body grows sick; death draws near; here come the friends and relations saying, "Make your will". And the sick man looks upon them and sees their weeping and is moved to evil and thinks within himself saying: "Lo, I put my soul and body and all that I have into your hands!" That man is truly accursed, who trusteth and layeth his body and soul and all that he hath in such hands as these: as the Lord saith through the prophet: "Cursed is he that trusteth in man!" Then they send for the priest. The priest saith: "Wilt thou take penance for all thy sins?" "Yea", saith he. "Wilt thou make satisfaction for what thou hast done, and for whatsoever fraud or deceit thou hast wrought to men, as best thou canst, from out of thy substance?" "Nay", saith he. "Why not?" saith the priest. "Because I have committed all to the hands of my kinsfolk and friends." And with this he begins to lose the power of speech, and so the poor wretch dies...and the devil seizes upon his soul and bears it off from the body with such anguish and tribulation as no man can conceive but he who suffers it.... And his kinsfolk and friends will bear off and divide his substance; and then they will say: "Curses on the fellow's soul; for he might have gotten more than he did, and have given it to us!" Meanwhile the worms gnaw upon his body; and thus he loseth both body and soul in this transitory world, and will go to hell, to be tormented world without end.

A passage like this helps us to understand how the Franciscans became the greatest mission-preachers of the Middle Ages, with their power of appealing to the popular belief in the directest and simplest language. This complements that other side of their preaching, in which they pleaded and enlarged upon all that Christ had suffered for men's souls, with the passionate urgency of disciples who had themselves trodden the winepress with Christ. And it also helps to explain Francis's horror of heresy, and the considerable part taken by later Franciscans, after the Dominicans, in the activities of the Inquisition.

In this, Francis was a man of his age, and he was thoroughly medieval also in his trust to catastrophic revolution. For good or for evil, it is more difficult for the propagandist to move an educated nation; this needs long and careful organization. But Francis's peasant-creed appealed to the Italian peasantry with the inevitable force of Rousseau's appeal to the Social Contract and the Noble Savage, or of the Soviet appeal in modern Russia; moreover, many nobles and intellectuals soon fell in with the movement. To them it was a great renunciation of worldly things. It is false to suppose that Franciscans were the ordinary attendants at leper-hospitals: such cases are not commonly recorded even in the earliest days, nor recorded at all, I believe, in later centuries. But their general renunciation was very great; and, in the first days, it involved a very considerable sacrifice even to the average peasant. In that essential particular, it differed widely from all other movements of equal force in medieval or modern Europe: the revolutions of 1789 and 1917 called upon the peasant to endow himself, Francis called upon him to despoil himself. And that is one reason why the Franciscan movement still means so much to the modern world, in spite of its considerable failures in its own day.

I have described elsewhere very plainly—indeed, if I am to believe some of my critics, with unfair emphasis—the failure of the friars in some of their main objects.[1] The emphasis would certainly have been unfair, as certain parts of this present work would be disproportionate and unfair, if it had not been necessary to correct the still greater one-sidedness of those who think to do God service by refusing to admit human weaknesses in a saint and his work, and who flood the book-market and the magazines with fancy history. In this chapter, I need only point out briefly the failure of what may be called St Francis's frontal

[1] *From St Francis to Dante, passim*; *Ten Medieval Studies* (no. 9, *The Failure of the Friars*, reprinted from *The Hibbert Journal* of January, 1907).

attack upon capitalism. His exaggerations there were as fatal as have been the exaggerations of any other revolutionary, before or since. Capitalism was a strong and growing force, in Italy especially, when Francis preached; yet no economic historian, I believe, has produced documentary evidence for any check in that growth. On the other hand, medieval friars of the second and third generations plainly describe the increase, rather than decrease, of usury; and certainly medieval Italy possessed most usurers and merchant-princes in the days when friars were most numerous. Francis made the mistake of the modern out-and-out pacifist; he did not realize how long the good spirit must be fostered before the corresponding evil spirit can be driven out. Ideally, it is intolerable that one man should wallow in superfluity amid a starving multitude, as it is intolerable that men should be organized for mutual slaughter. But the disbanding of a wicked soldiery does not at once create good citizens; and, in the other field, there is much truth in Dr Johnson's saying that a man is seldom more innocently employed than when he is making money. Hitherto, the peoples which have not organized for war have generally dealt still more barbarously with human life in disorganized detail; again, those which have not evolved capitalism are those which have not had

the wits or the energy to evolve it. Francis had
no more opportunity for generalizing thus than he
had for realizing a Christian faith independent of
the material heaven and the material hell; his
headlong attack upon capitalism was a Charge of
the Light Brigade. Worse still, his followers often
became capitalists, in a small but comfortable way,
under a false cloak of desti-
tution. Erasmus is only one
of many critics who exposed
the hollow fiction by which
Franciscans, forbidden to
touch money, would count
their gains with a stick or
with gloved hands; and Hol-
bein seized upon this for
one of his marginal sketches
to the *Praise of Folly* (chapter
54). We have already seen
how, less than a century

Fig. 10. Friar counting
with a stick, by Hol-
bein.

after Francis's death, four of his friars were publicly
burned at Marseilles for adhering with heretical
obstinacy to their Master's first ideal of poverty.
Moreover, to some extent it became obvious to
the majority even of St Francis's best disciples
that the saint's abdication of possessions had been
too extreme. Complete poverty, in the earliest
Franciscan sense, would have condemned the

Order to ignorance also, and nothing did so much to encourage juggling with the Rule—nothing contributed so fatally to break down the Rule in practice while it was left standing in theory—as the irresistible attraction which brought the friars to the universities, and which made them for more than a century the best of university students and teachers. While, therefore, it is true that the friar accustomed society to the idea of voluntary poverty, and thus removed much of the mere snobbish stigma attaching to lack of means, yet it is also true that some friars, for their part, familiarized the world with the spectacle of idleness and hypocrisy masquerading as self-denial. Yet, when all allowances have been made, there remains a very definite balance on the good side. In the earlier thirteenth century, it was common enough for a knight, a rich merchant, or a great ecclesiastic, to have a son or a brother among the Mendicants; later, it was still more common for a distinguished university teacher to be a Mendicant himself. The knight or judge might not share his brother's ideas about poverty—he might even, with part of his mind, despise such ideas as pusillanimous—but at the back even of the most unsympathetic mind there would remain a real impression of something attempted, something done by the friar, which, on searching our own hearts, we cannot certainly say that we ourselves would have the courage to imitate. To that extent, for two or three generations at least, the direct attack may be pronounced a success. Again, while the friars' renunciation did something real everywhere to render poverty more respectable, it exercised in some quarters considerable indirect force. It set up a practical moral standard to which the older Orders must to some extent conform, or lose religious and moral prestige; for, to the very end, the friar had not only less financial security, but also a smaller income, than the average monk; and therefore, to the very end, he could maintain even this lower financial position only by showing, or seeming to show, that he was giving society value for their money. The rise of the friars, while delaying in some directions the movements for Church reform, stimulated them in others. If the sixteenth century was far better prepared for an enduring religious change than the thirteenth had been, a good deal of this progress must be put to the credit of the friars.

Moreover, even though the direct failure had been greater, it would be difficult to regret in Francis that chivalrous exaggeration which has left the inspiration of such wonderful self-sacrifice. We must remember what may be the slow and cumulative effect of some striking action which, from the immediate and superficial point of view, may have been condemned as a startling failure. The world has never forgotten Francis: for seven centuries social reformers have drawn direct inspiration from his life and words; and, though at certain times and in certain countries the saint's star has suffered eclipse, yet the revival of interest in this present generation is very remarkable. It had already begun before Sabatier's epoch-making work; and one of the most startling features of this revival is its strength in Protestant countries and in unsacerdotal circles. This is most easily stated, and can be very fairly represented, in terms of published literature. Quite apart from modern lives and histories, a single English publisher, in the last 20 years, has issued translations of five of the most important original Franciscan sources, and the aggregate sale of these five, during that period, amounts to nearly 100,000 copies. This would be considerably swelled by the sales of other publishers, and it is extremely doubtful whether the whole of the rest of Europe has bought as much as this of vernacular Franciscan sources. Moreover, among all these thousands of readers, many are intensely interested in the poverty-problem, not only from an historical but from the most modern and practical point of view. Mr H. G. Wells, in an article on *Labour after the War*, told how many rich men of his acquaintance were adopting, quite naturally, the point of view that they are only trustees for what they possess—public officials from the ethical point of view, though not in the eye of the law—public officials administering their great factory or their hereditary estates in the public interest as well as in their own, claiming for themselves a good salary, but desiring no more than this, and preferring to invest the residue in the improvement of the concern rather than to spend it on themselves. And men are becoming more and more familiarized with similar ideas from a more definitely spiritual point of view. Our grandfathers, when materialistically minded, treated attacks upon existing laws of property as a negation of human justice: when religiously minded, as impious. The tendency now is rather to welcome such changes in the name both of justice and of religion. And the mere survival of the original mustard-seed of Franciscanism through seven centuries, even though no grain of it had ever germinated in the interval, might conceivably some day become a decisive factor in human civilization. It might, in such favourable soil as the present, stimulate a sudden growth such as mankind might otherwise have awaited in vain for many centuries. In history, two contrary factors seem equally remarkable; first, the immense time often required for the growth of a movement; and again the almost miraculous suddenness of its final expansion, when the long period of silent growth is finished.

Again, it is no mere paradox to say that the Franciscan idea may be as fruitful today in its failure as in its success. If a teacher tells us what he really thinks, we learn more even by disagreement with him than by agreement with a half-hearted man. Whenever, again, a man's actions have been sincere in the past, and he has staked his very life on them, his example stimulates us, by attraction or by repulsion, immeasurably beyond the stimulus of mere passive discipleship. Therefore history is morally justified in the most unsparing analysis of great men's motives and actions. First, the great men themselves would have had it so: in proportion to their real greatness, they invite us not to forget the very warts upon their face. And secondly, only so can we fully profit by their greatness. It is only by an elaborate process of trigonometry that we can infer the present or the future from the past, even with approximate correctness. On the one hand, we must measure the whole height of the personal greatness of St Francis; on the other, the whole extent of his failures in public work: only thus can we pass on to measure what must have been lacking in his methods, as applied to the society of his day. And the failure of Franciscan-Dominican mendicancy, even in its own age, was greater than is commonly represented. Their example had no very directly traceable effect even on the older Orders or on the secular clergy. Yet, with all these failures, it was a magnificent movement, fraught with enduring results; and it was a definite forward step for democracy. We can read this even through Chaucer's satire, and it is admirably brought out by Dr A. G. Little.[1] Francis was right; the Lord had revealed to him a way, if not better in itself than St Benedict's, most certainly better as a corrective to certain tendencies in later Benedictinism.

[1] *Studies in English Franciscan History*, 1917, pp. 53, 98.

INDEX

Abailard, 1, 10, 70; and study of theology, 91 92; *and see* St Bernard
Abbacies, 41
Abbot, difficulties of, 46; duties of, 47
Abbots, and Bible-study, 85; building by, 73; and leave to wander, 85
Abraham, 98
Accidia, 93, 107
Adam, 87, 98
Alaric, 68
Alexander III, Pope, 79
Ambrose, St, 15
Anchorites, 61
Angelica hilaritas, 67
Animals, 8; conversion of wolf, 74; *and see* St Bernard
Anse, Étienne d', 77
Anti-Catholicism, 75
Antichrist, 59
Anticlericalism, 72
Apocalypse, 95
Apostacy, 43; Joachim accused of, 85
Architecture, Art, 70, 71; Catholic, 63
Aristotle, 72
Armageddon, 59
Arnulf, *see* Boyers
Augustinians, 100

Bábí creed, 87 n.
Babylon, 68, 97
Bacon, Roger, 15
Baxter, 67

Beds, feather, 74
Beghards, 82, 83
Béguines, 82, 83
Bégule, M. Lucien, 71 n.
Benedictine ideal, 62
Benedictines, 1 n., 121; decay of, 94, Joachim on, 94; poverty-ideal of, 89; and universities, 2
Benedictinism, later, 121
Bible (medieval), in French, 80; and heresy, 16; study, 85, 93, 119 (*and see* Monasteries, St Bernard); struggle for open, 78 ff.; Waldo's translation of, 77
Bilson, J., 71 n.
Bishop, and property, 74
Bondmen, 74
Booth, General, 110 n.
Bourbon, Étienne de, 14, 76, 77, 79
Boyers, Arnulf of, 33
Brakelonde, Jocelin of, 46
Brescia, Arnold of, 3
Brother Body, 110
Browne, Prof. E. G., 87 n.
Buffon, 5
Bunyan, 16, 67
Burgundian, Burgundians, 6; architecture, 71 n.
Burgundy, 5

Cain, 43
Calabria, 84, 93; reformed Cistercians in, 85
Cambrensis, Giraldus, 28
Canon Law, 49

123

INDEX

www.ingramcontent.com/pod-product-compliance
Ingram Content Group UK Ltd.
Pitfield, Milton Keynes, MK11 3LW, UK
UKHW042146280225
455719UK00001B/142